BATTLE
AGAINST
ULTRON

Written by Matt Forbeck

Senior Editor Sadie Smith
Senior Designer Robert Perry
Editors Lauren Nesworthy, Julia March
Pre-Production Producer Siu Yin Chan
Producer David Appleyard
Managing Editor Laura Gilbert
Managing Art Editor Maxine Pedliham
Art Director Lisa Lanzarini
Publisher Julie Ferris
Publishing Director Simon Beecroft

Design and additional text Dynamo Limited

First published in Great Britain in 2015
by Dorling Kindersley Limited
80 Strand, London WC2R 0RL
A Penguin Random House Company

10 9 8 7 6 5 4 3 2 1

001–270980–Mar/2015

© 2015 MARVEL

A CIP catalogue record for this book
is available from the British Library.

ISBN: 978-0-24100-763-1

Colour reproduction by Alta Image Ltd, UK
Printed and bound by South China Printing Company Ltd.

www.dk.com

A WORLD OF IDEAS
SEE ALL THERE IS TO KNOW

Contents

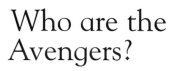

Who are the Avengers?

The Avengers are the mightiest team of Super Heroes on Earth. They first joined together when the heroes Thor and the Hulk were caught up in the evil schemes of Loki, the god of trickery. When Ant-Man, Wasp and Iron Man also became involved, the heroes all banded together to defeat the wicked Super Villain.

As a team, the heroes were successful. Ant-Man suggested that they should stay together to face future enemies too powerful to tackle alone. Wasp came up with the name the "Avengers", and so an unbeatable team of Super Heroes was created! The legendary Captain America soon joined the team and became their leader.

Over the years, the team has attracted even more Super Heroes from far and wide, each of them eager to have the honour of being called an Avenger. Together, the heroes have saved Earth countless times. They have fought the most dangerous villains, from the killer robot Ultron to the terrifying Titan Thanos.

No matter what threatens the world, the Avengers always rise to the challenge. If they cannot save everyone, they can at least avenge them! Avengers assemble!

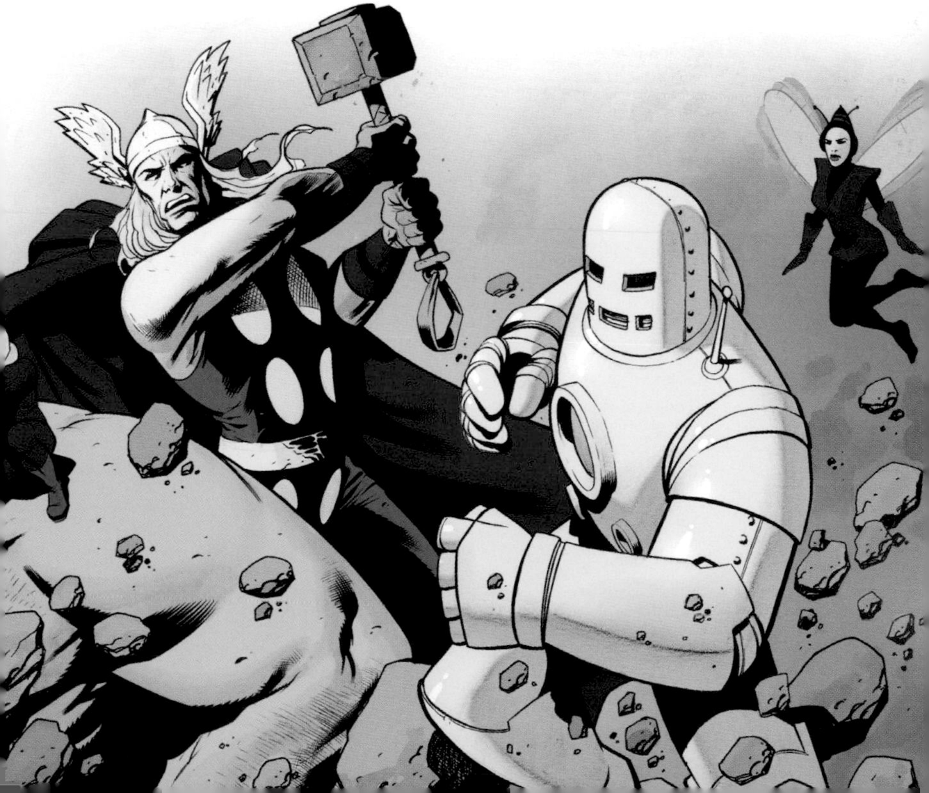

AVENGERS
FACT FILE

Iron Man, Ant-Man, Wasp, Thor and the Hulk were the founding members of the Avengers. Captain America joined after being discovered trapped in ice, then Hawkeye became part of the line-up. Vision joined the team later.

CAPTAIN AMERICA

Real name: Steve Rogers
Occupation: Adventurer,
S.H.I.E.L.D. operative, team
leader of the Avengers
Powers/skills:
Enhanced strength, speed
and endurance. Expert boxer,
trained in martial arts.

IRON MAN

Real name: Anthony "Tony" Stark
Occupation: Businessman
Powers/skills: Genius inventor. Tony's standard Iron Man armour gives him extra strength and speed, and even the ability to fly.

THOR

Real name: Thor Odinson
Occupation: Prince of Asgard, god of thunder
Powers/skills: Strength and endurance of a god, with an extended lifespan. Can control thunder and lightning.

THE HULK

Real name: Robert Bruce Banner
Occupation: Scientist
Powers/skills: Limitless strength and endurance. Can leap several miles in one bound. Body heals from wounds almost instantly.

HAWKEYE

Real name: Clint Barton
Occupation: Outlaw adventurer, former circus performer
Powers/skills: World-class marksman with incredible reflexes and hand-eye coordination. Natural athlete and formidable unarmed combatant.

WASP

Real name: Janet van Dyne
Occupation: Adventurer
Powers/skills: Flies at speeds
up to 64 kmph (40 mph).
Can alter her size using Pym
Particles, shrinking to the size
of an insect or growing as
tall as a building.

ANT-MAN

Real name:
Henry "Hank" Pym
Occupation:
Biochemist
Powers/skills: Can
reduce himself down to
the size of an ant. His
helmet allows him to
communicate with ants.

VISION

Real name: Vision
Occupation: Adventurer
Powers/skills: Can
change his body mass at
will. Able to blast solar
energy from his eyes and
from the jewel on his
brow. Superhuman
intelligence and strength.

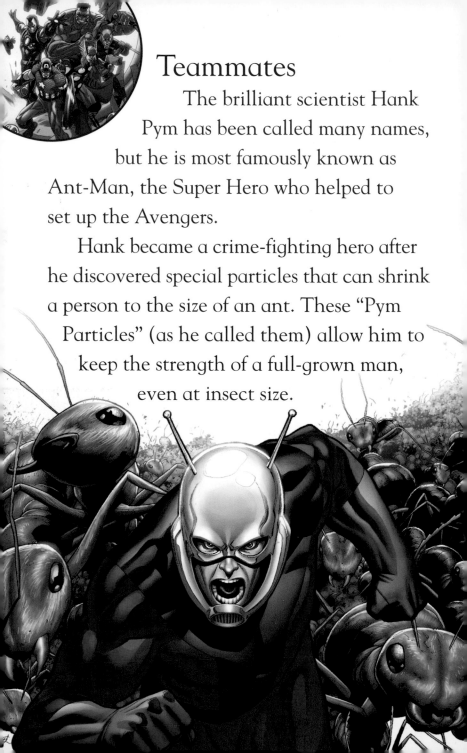

Teammates

The brilliant scientist Hank Pym has been called many names, but he is most famously known as Ant-Man, the Super Hero who helped to set up the Avengers.

Hank became a crime-fighting hero after he discovered special particles that can shrink a person to the size of an ant. These "Pym Particles" (as he called them) allow him to keep the strength of a full-grown man, even at insect size.

Hank also built a helmet that helps him communicate with ants. He uses the ants to gather information that helps him defeat villains. Sometimes, Ant-Man even rides a flying ant for a quick getaway!

As well as fighting alongside the Avengers, Hank spends much of his time making scientific discoveries and inventing amazing devices. It was this love of inventing that led to Hank creating Ultron, an intelligent and powerful robot. Sadly, Ultron turned against his creator and became a truly evil villain. He is determined to destroy Earth, and the Avengers have battled him many times.

Ant-Man is desperate to make up for having created Ultron, and is continually searching for a way to destroy him once and for all.

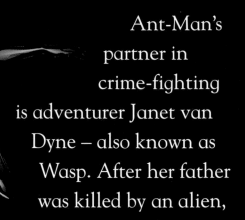

Ant-Man's partner in crime-fighting is adventurer Janet van Dyne – also known as Wasp. After her father was killed by an alien, Janet wanted the power to avenge him, so she asked Ant-Man for help. He used his Pym Particles to give her the ability to shrink to the size of an insect and grow wings. She decided to use her new powers to fight crime, calling herself Wasp. She often uses her skills as a fashion designer to come up with a variety of incredible costumes, and she is also excellent at organising and planning missions. Occasionally, she has even acted as the leader of the Avengers.

The true leader of the Avengers, however, has always been Captain America. This legendary hero has kept the team together through the toughest of times. Before he turned into the Super Soldier he is today, Captain America was a sickly young man named Steve Rogers. During World War II, Steve volunteered to take part in a secret government experiment. He took a special serum, and was transformed into a strong and powerful soldier. Steve was given a red, white and blue costume, as well as a virtually indestructible shield, and became the incredible Super Hero, Captain America. Along with his sidekick and friend, Bucky, Cap fought many battles against the Nazis and the evil organisation known as Hydra.

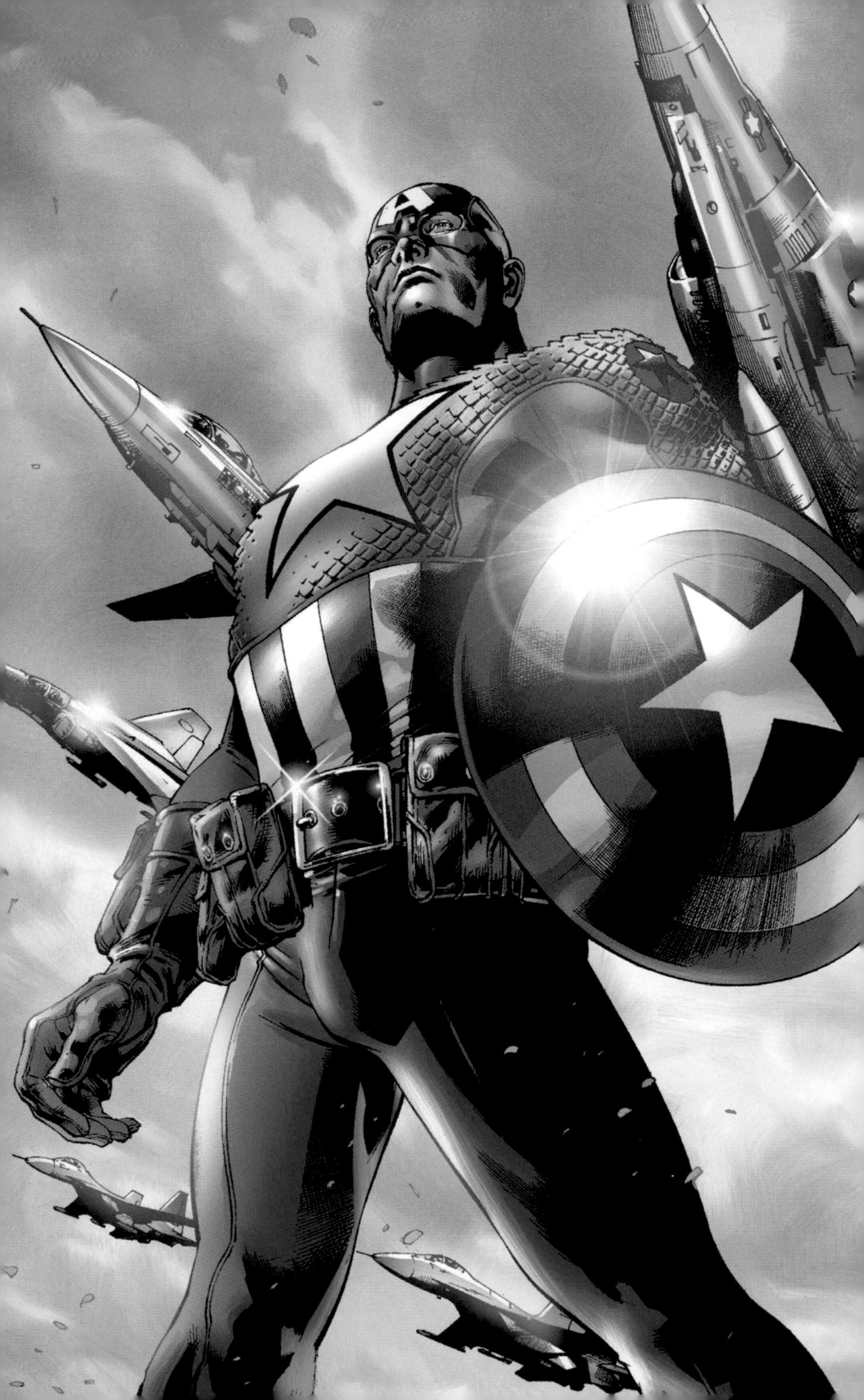

While on an Army mission, Cap fell into the ocean and was frozen in a block of ice. Many years later, the Avengers found him – still alive! The world had changed, but Cap remained as steadfast as ever. The Avengers respect their fearless leader, as he always believes in standing up for what's right.

But Captain America is not alone – he often shares leadership with Iron Man. Genius billionaire Tony Stark used to invent weapons for the US Army. While testing one of them in Afghanistan, he was wounded in an explosion and had shrapnel lodged dangerously near his heart. He was captured by warlords, who forced him to make weapons for them. Instead, Tony secretly built an incredible iron suit of armour!

DAILY BUGLE EXCLUSIVE STOP PRESS!

When a Super-Soldier Serum was given to Steve Rogers, it increased his size, strength and endurance to almost superhuman levels. As Captain America, he fought alongside the army until he was lost at sea during a mission and presumed dead.

DAILY BUGLE

FOUND!

IS THIS THE REAL CAPTAIN AMERICA?

By our special Super Hero Correspondent

DAILY BUGLE

In an exciting discovery, the Avengers have found a man frozen in a block of ice in the North Atlantic Ocean. Could this be Captain America, the famous World War II Super Hero who disappeared in 1944?

The Avengers discovered the frozen block of ice while hunting for Prince Namor of Atlantis. They thawed out the block and discovered the man inside was still alive.

"We are waiting for him to wake up," Iron Man said in an exclusive phone interview. "He is wearing a Stars-and-Stripes costume, and Thor is convinced that the mysterious man's shield is indestructible."

"It looks like he has been frozen in the ice block for decades!" added Wasp. "We are hoping that this is indeed Captain America. We will know soon enough."

Tony's armour protected his heart, and gave him enough strength and speed to escape his captors. When he was a free man, he decided to give up making weapons and transformed himself into the Super Hero Iron Man instead!

As Iron Man, Tony has battled many villains alongside the Avengers, and uses his great wealth to fund the team. He loves technology, and he is always building better versions of his armour as well as new gadgets for his teammates.

Tony Stark is a true genius and one of the greatest inventors of high-tech equipment. However, Doctor Bruce Banner comes close to equalling him in terms of intelligence.

Like Tony, this brilliant scientist developed weapons for the army, including a dangerous gamma bomb. When the bomb was being tested, a teenager accidentally wandered onto the test site. Bruce rushed out to save him and was able to push the boy out of the way in time. However, it was too late for the scientist – he was bombarded by gamma rays! They caused a mutation that turned Bruce into a gigantic, green monster called the Hulk. Now, the Hulk appears whenever Bruce gets angry, and he has unimaginable power. He can travel miles with a single jump, and bullets bounce off his super-tough skin.

Despite all the good things that the Hulk has done as a Super Hero, many people are afraid of his rage and sheer strength. Because of this, the Hulk prefers to be alone, often staying away from the people he cares about in order to avoid hurting them by accident. Sometimes, this even includes the other Avengers.

Thor, the Norse god of thunder however, is not afraid of the Hulk. He is perhaps the only Avenger who has battled the Hulk and even come close to winning.

Before becoming an Avenger, Thor lived as a mighty warrior prince in the beautiful realm of Asgard. Thor loved his people, but his father, King Odin, thought he was too proud to rule the kingdom wisely. Odin 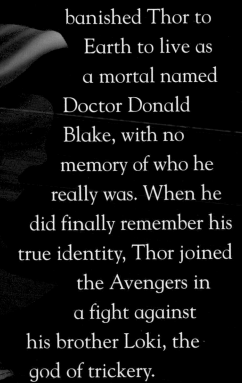 banished Thor to Earth to live as a mortal named Doctor Donald Blake, with no memory of who he really was. When he did finally remember his true identity, Thor joined the Avengers in a fight against his brother Loki, the god of trickery.

WHO WOULD YOU FOLLOW?

Captain America and Iron Man are both capable leaders of the Avengers, but when it comes to commanding a team of Super Heroes, their leadership qualities are very different.

> **"MY JOB IS TO MAKE TOMORROW'S WORLD BETTER. ALWAYS HAS BEEN."**

CAPTAIN AMERICA

Cap is courageous and disciplined. His military experience and tactical skills mean there is no one better to lead the Avengers into battle.

KEY STRENGTHS

- Extreme agility, strength and speed
- Phenomenal endurance
- Experienced at battle strategy
- Indestructible Vibranium shield
- One of the most skilled human combatants on Earth

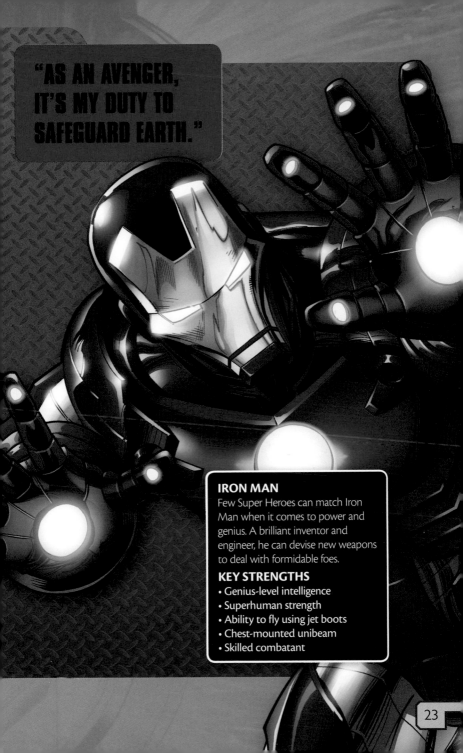

"AS AN AVENGER, IT'S MY DUTY TO SAFEGUARD EARTH."

IRON MAN

Few Super Heroes can match Iron Man when it comes to power and genius. A brilliant inventor and engineer, he can devise new weapons to deal with formidable foes.

KEY STRENGTHS

- Genius-level intelligence
- Superhuman strength
- Ability to fly using jet boots
- Chest-mounted unibeam
- Skilled combatant

23

Since that first battle against Loki,
Thor has become one of the most powerful
Avengers. As the god of thunder, he can use
his mighty hammer, Mjolnir, to create great
storms and to summon blasts of lightning to
defeat his enemies. Thor has grown to love
Earth and its people, and he has sworn to
protect it always. He has, like all the other
Avengers, been a great inspiration to people.

Clint Barton was inspired to become
a hero after seeing Iron Man in action.

When he was just 14, Clint ran away to join the circus. During his time there, he learned amazing acrobatics and trained to become the world's greatest archer. He called himself Hawkeye and prepared himself for a life as a Super Hero. Unfortunately, things didn't go quite as he had planned.

The first time Clint tried to stop a robbery, he was mistaken for a thief. A spy called Black Widow saved him from the police and convinced him to work with her, against Iron Man. However, he was unhappy being a criminal, so Jarvis helped him meet the Avengers. Iron Man persuaded Cap that Clint deserved a chance with the team. Hawkeye proved himself to be a worthy Avenger!

Hawkeye also convinced Black Widow to join the team of heroes. Black Widow's real name is Natasha Romanova, and she used to be one of the greatest spies in the world. She was sent to spy on Tony Stark and steal his company's secrets. After fighting Iron Man several times, Black Widow decided to change sides and join the Avengers.

Like Cap, Black Widow was also given a Super-Soldier Serum that turned her into a perfect athlete. It protects her from illnesses and poisons and keeps her body fit and strong. As a former ballerina, Black Widow is also very agile and as a former spy, she has great intelligence. She has everything it takes to be a great Avenger!

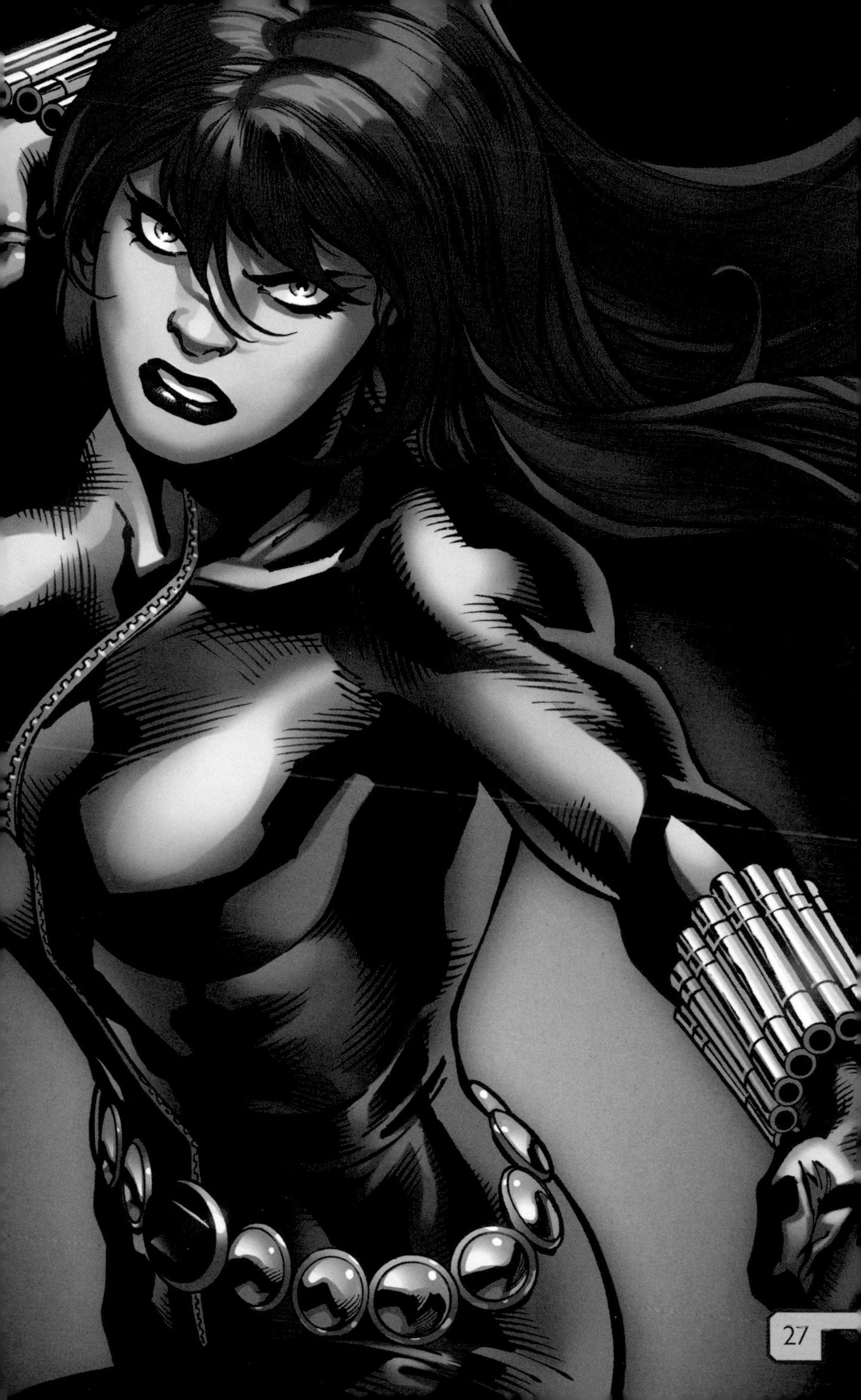

THE AVENGERS CHARTER

When the founding Avengers first came together as a team, they decided to create and sign the Avengers Charter. This official document contains a list of rules that every member must swear to live by.

- The Avengers must protect Earth from any threat.

- All Avengers must use their powers for good causes.

- The Avengers should meet at least once a week.

- Each Avenger is allowed to have a secret identity.

- Any new member of the Avengers must have at least one special skill or power.

- Each Avenger must respect the others and work well in a team.

- Avengers must always answer the call: Avengers Assemble!

Signed:

....

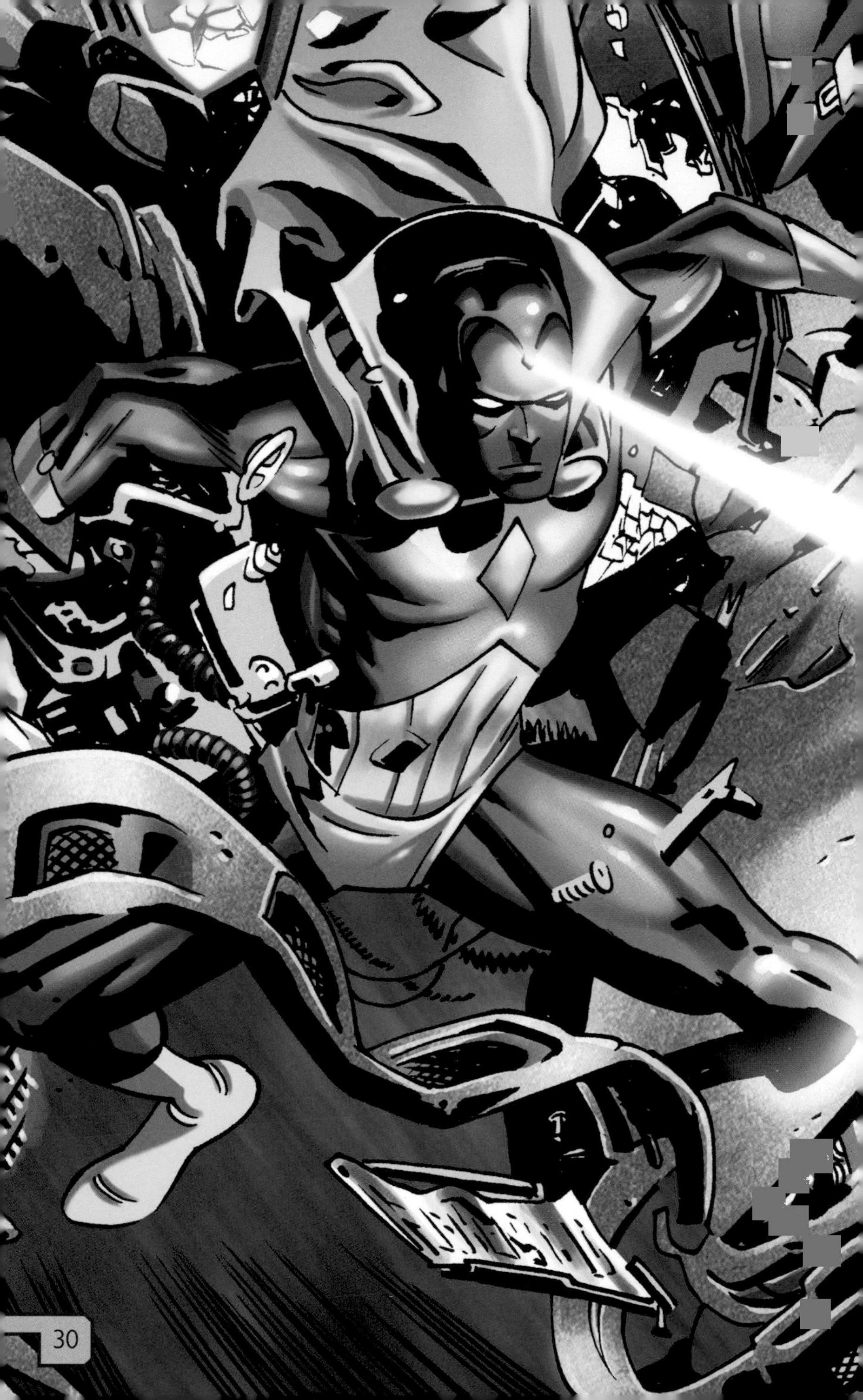

Black Widow is not the only villain to transform herself into a hero. Vision was an android created by the evil robot Ultron to destroy the Avengers. However, like Ultron did before him, Vision turned against his creator. He fought against his programming and chose to work alongside the heroes.

Vision is a very powerful Avenger. His brain can communicate with computers. He can also make his body become harder than diamonds, or ghostlike, so that he can walk through anything – even other people!

Vision has been destroyed and rebuilt a number of times, but he always returns to fight another day with the Avengers.

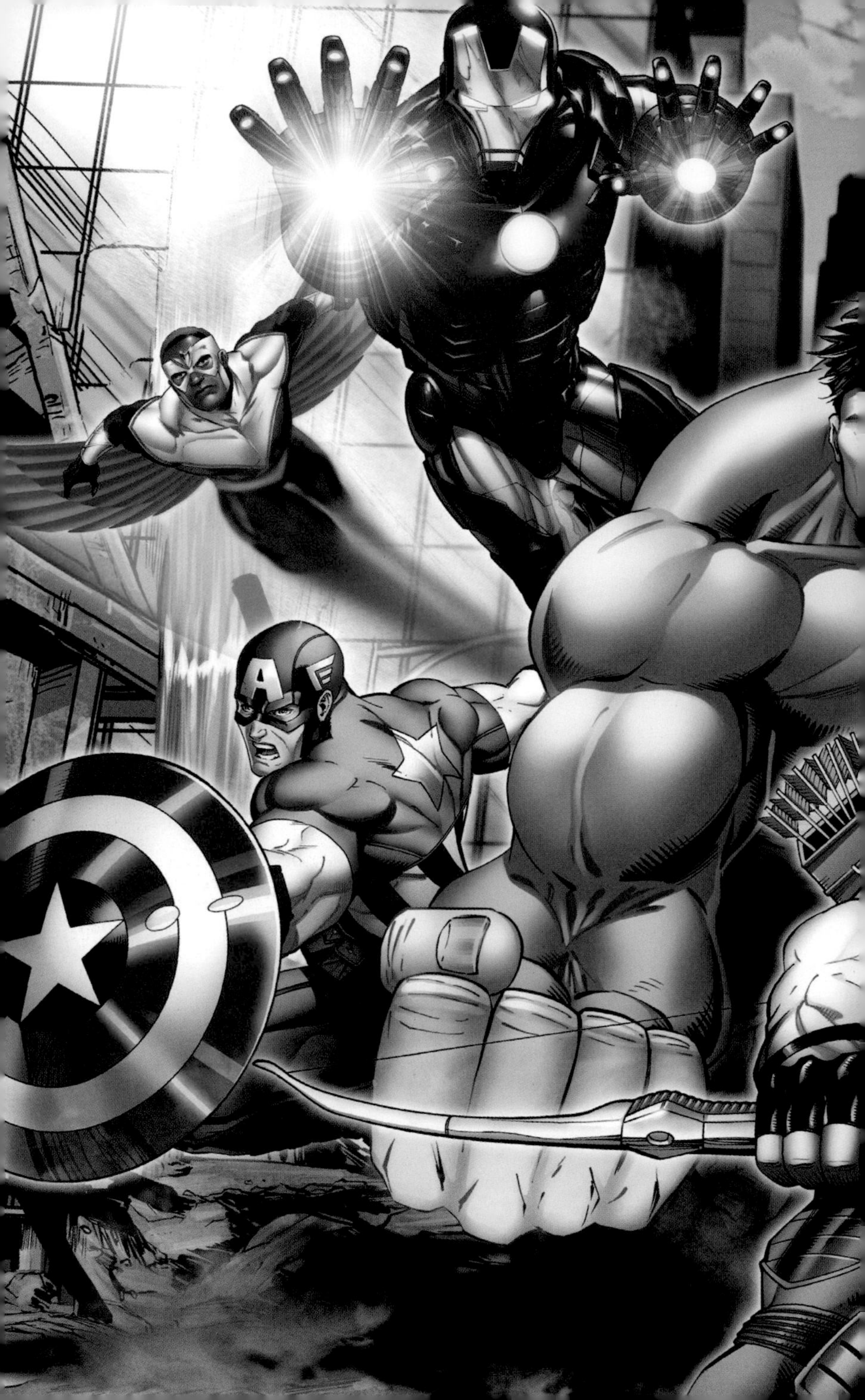

The Avengers are an awesome team of Super Heroes who work together to fight evil, wherever it might be.

Superpowers and Gear

The call to assemble could come at any time, so the Avengers have to keep themselves in top physical condition. They are always ready to take down any Super Villain and protect Earth! Many of them spend countless hours training in the gym at the Avengers headquarters to improve and maintain their strength, speed and endurance.

Captain America, Hawkeye and Black Widow are all experts in acrobatics and martial arts. They have mastered many types of hand-to-hand combat, from boxing to jujitsu. Ant-Man and Wasp use their tiny size to their advantage, by quickly striking any weak points before their larger opponents even know what hit them!

The android Vision doesn't need to train to improve his strength or endurance. He has the incredible ability increase his body's density so that it is harder than steel.

As an Asgardian god, Thor has a tough and dense body, made of pure muscle. He is strong enough to carve stone with his bare fingers! When Thor needs even more power, he can wear a magical belt called Megingjord, which doubles his strength.

Strongest of them all, the giant, muscly Hulk towers over the mighty Thor. He can lift just about anything, even an entire mountain! If the Hulk is attacked, he becomes angrier, which only makes him stronger. No man-made weapon has ever taken him down – his strength makes him practically indestructible.

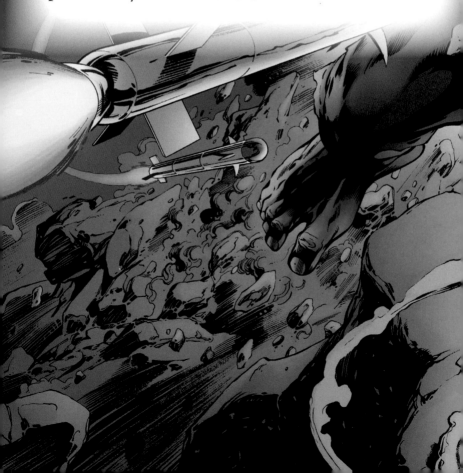

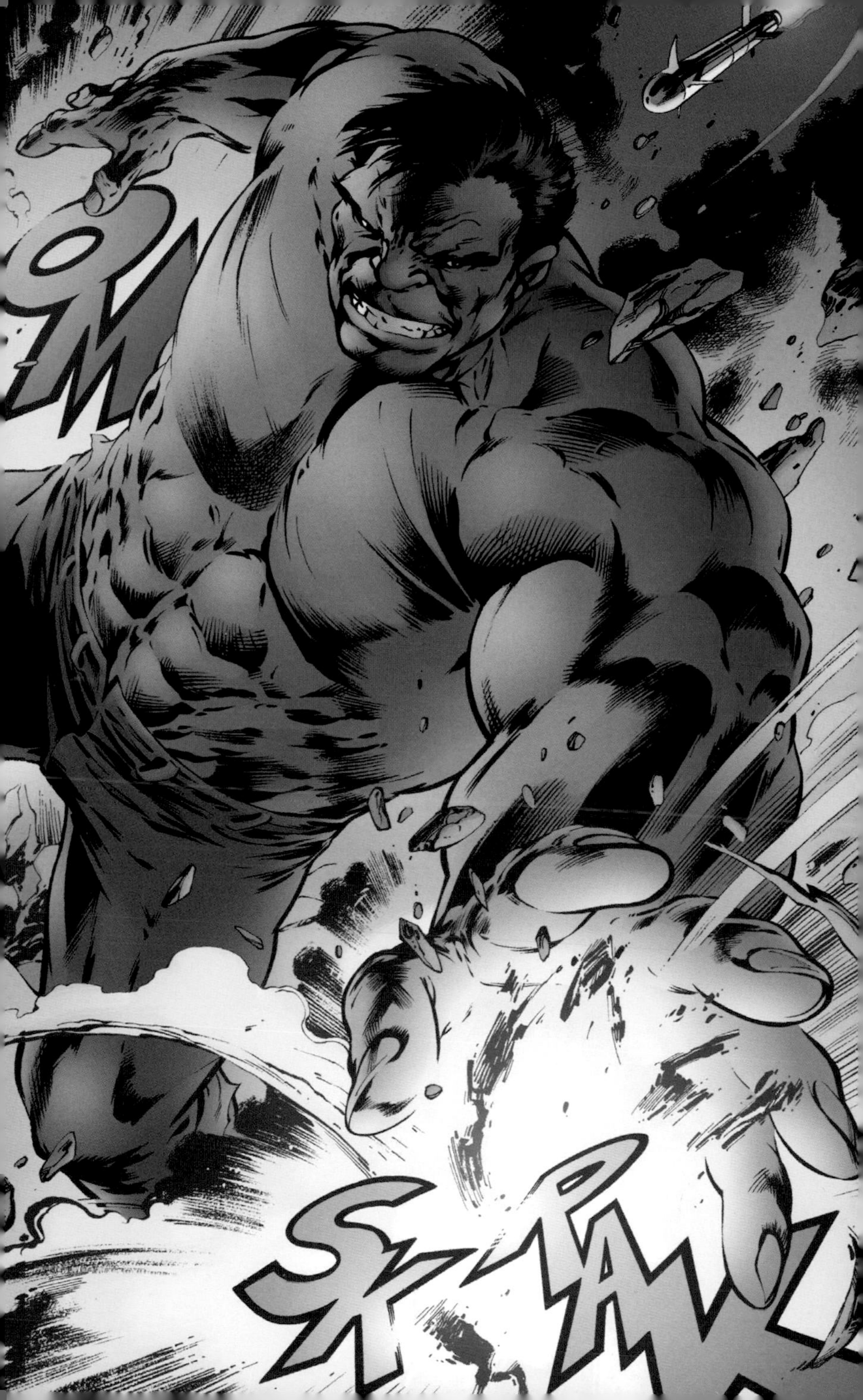
OM

MAN or MONSTER?

Scientist Bruce Banner was accidentally bombarded by gamma rays. Now, whenever his heart rate speeds up, he transforms into an enormous, muscly, green monster called the Incredible Hulk.

"LOOK, I'M WARNING YOU FOR YOUR OWN SAKES, DON'T MAKE ME MAD."

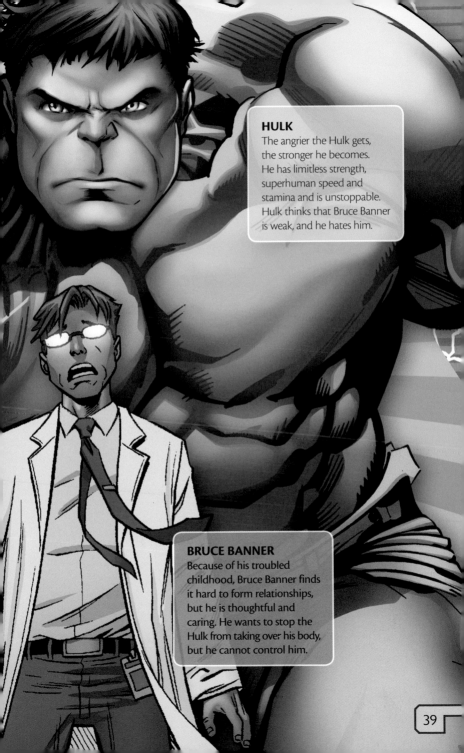

HULK
The angrier the Hulk gets, the stronger he becomes. He has limitless strength, superhuman speed and stamina and is unstoppable. Hulk thinks that Bruce Banner is weak, and he hates him.

BRUCE BANNER
Because of his troubled childhood, Bruce Banner finds it hard to form relationships, but he is thoughtful and caring. He wants to stop the Hulk from taking over his body, but he cannot control him.

However, strength alone is not always enough. Many Avengers need weapons to give them the edge in a fight. Hawkeye is a master with a bow and arrow – he never misses a shot. He also uses all kinds of "trick" arrows against his enemies, which can deliver bursts of acid, electric shocks, nets and even explosions!

Vision's best weapon is created by his own artificial body. He absorbs energy from the sun, and then uses that energy to fire powerful blasts from the jewel on his forehead.

Black Widow and Wasp both have weapons that can knock down a foe with an electric shock. Wasp generates the blasts of energy for her lethal sting from her own body, while Black Widow shoots powerful Widow's Bites from bracelets on her wrists. These bracelets can also release small explosions, and a hook with a cable attached. Black Widow can use this to climb up buildings or swing from rooftops when making a daring escape from a dangerous situation.

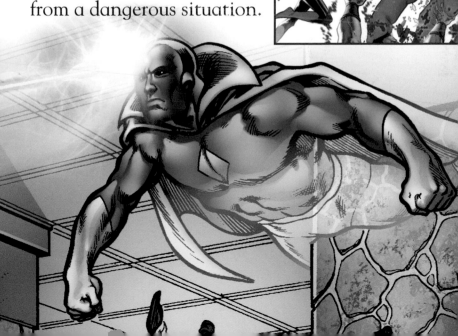

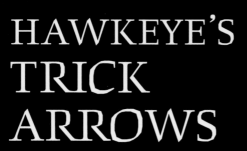

HAWKEYE'S TRICK ARROWS

Hawkeye, Earth's mightiest marksman, has no superhuman powers, but he is an exceptional archer. His aim is perfect from any angle, and he often uses a variety of "trick" arrows.

1. Tear gas arrow
Releases a concentrated cloud of tear gas

2. Putty arrow
Tipped with a bulb containing a sticky chemical that bursts on impact

3. Net arrow
Releases a 3-m- (10-ft-) wide net through the end of the shaft

4. Acid arrow
Attached to a tube of concentrated nitric acid that burns on impact

5. Sonic arrow
Emits a
high-pitched
95-decibel sound

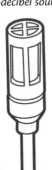

6. Bola arrow
Releases three balls
on 46-cm (18-in)
cables that wrap
around the target

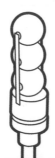

7. Explosive-tip arrow
Contains an
explosive that
detonates on
impact

8. Smoke bomb arrow
Emits thick clouds
of chemical smoke

Thor carries a very special weapon. He uses his magical hammer, Mjolnir, to create wild storms to make things harder for his enemies. No matter how far Thor throws the hammer, it will always return to him when he calls for it, even if it has to punch through a planet to reach him! Thor is the only one who can lift Mjolnir, so he is able to use it like a giant paperweight to pin villains to

the ground. That way, he can go battle
another foe and come back to deal with
the trapped enemy later.

Iron Man is able to equip his suits of
armour with all kinds of weapons, from bullets
to missiles. Every suit of armour can also fire
repulsor blasts from the palms of its hands.

Captain America often uses his shield
as a weapon. He can throw it for long
distances and bounce it off several targets
in a row. If he throws it at the
right angle, it will come
zooming back to
him, just like a
boomerang!

Although Captain America's shield makes a lethal weapon, its main purpose is to protect him. It was made with a special metal called Vibranium, which absorbs any impact and makes the shield almost indestructible. As long as Cap carries his shield, he can block any weapon or attack, no matter how strong!

Brilliant inventor Tony Stark relies on his armour to protect him in dangerous battles.

He constantly upgrades and improves his Iron Man suit, often adding spectacular new gadgets. He has gone through more than fifty different suits of armour and never runs out of ideas for amazing new designs.

Occasionally Tony builds special suits for specific purposes or environments. He even built a super-tough Hulkbuster armour, which is strong enough to protect Tony from blows from an angry Hulk!

Tony's armour doesn't just protect him – it also allows him to fly. The Iron Man suit has powerful jets built into the boots, which allow him to shoot through the air at up to five times the speed of sound. When he launches himself into the stars with a special suit built for space travel, he can reach other planets in no time at all.

IRON MAN'S ARMOUR

Iron Man's suits give him amazing strength, speed and, in later models, the ability to fly. He is always upgrading them to adapt to new circumstances.

MK II Golden Avenger

Equipped with a force field generator

MK IV Classic Gold and Red

Fitted with a hologram emitter

MK VII Silver Centurion

Has a protective force field

Uses solar power to recharge

War Machine

Has missiles and ballistic munitions

Hulkbuster Armour

Enhanced strength for combat with the Hulk

Hypervelocity Armour

Can operate without Tony inside

Travels at supersonic speed and underwater

An injection of experimental serum allows him to control his armour using his brain.

Coated armour for radar resistance

Powerful bomblets stored in gauntlets

A gold undersuit inside Tony's bones seeps out to connect the red external pieces.

Jet boots allow Iron Man to fly on Earth and in space.

Technology in the armour stops targeting systems from locking on to it.

Thor is able to fly by using his
hammer, Mjolnir. Holding tightly onto its
leather strap, Thor swings it in a circle until
he gains enough momentum to take off. He
then hurls it in the direction he wants to fly,
and it pulls him through the air.

Wasp is also able to fly. When she shrinks
down, a pair of tiny but strong wings appears
on her back. These wings, combined with
her size, allow her access to small spaces that
other Avengers could not reach.

When the rest of the Avengers need to get somewhere fast together, they jump aboard the team's Quinjet. This special plane is large enough to hold the Avengers who cannot fly, and it travels at twice the speed of sound. It can get every Super Hero to the scene of a battle in a flash!

AVENGERS
QUINJET

Supersonic speed and ultra-powerful weapons make the Quinjet the perfect transport and aerial combat vehicle for the world's foremost team of Super Heroes.

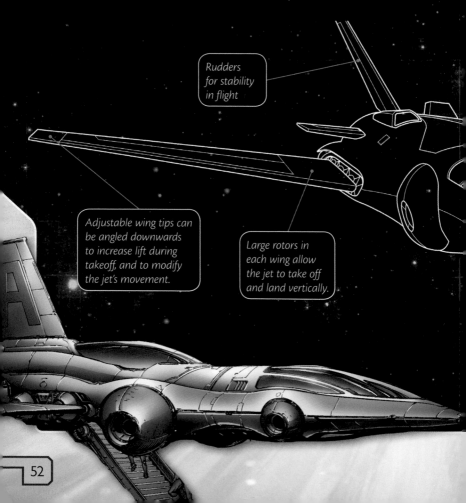

Rudders for stability in flight

Adjustable wing tips can be angled downwards to increase lift during takeoff, and to modify the jet's movement.

Large rotors in each wing allow the jet to take off and land vertically.

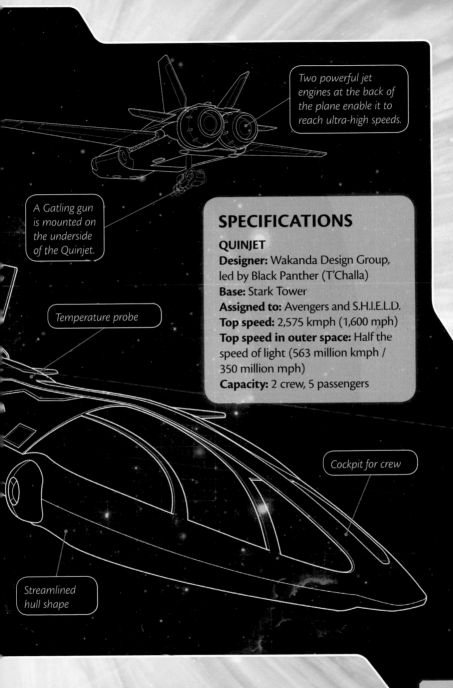

Two powerful jet engines at the back of the plane enable it to reach ultra-high speeds.

A Gatling gun is mounted on the underside of the Quinjet.

Temperature probe

SPECIFICATIONS

QUINJET
Designer: Wakanda Design Group, led by Black Panther (T'Challa)
Base: Stark Tower
Assigned to: Avengers and S.H.I.E.L.D.
Top speed: 2,575 kmph (1,600 mph)
Top speed in outer space: Half the speed of light (563 million kmph / 350 million mph)
Capacity: 2 crew, 5 passengers

Cockpit for crew

Streamlined hull shape

Enemies of the Avengers

From their very beginning, the Avengers have faced some of the most evil and clever villains the world has ever seen. That includes not just human wrongdoers, but also alien attackers from space and ancient gods looking for trouble.

Loki, the Norse god of trickery, was the Avengers' very first foe, but this mischief-maker was already very well known to one member of the team. Loki had been a problem for his brother Thor since they were both young gods in Asgard.

Loki was the son of the King of the Frost Giants, but unlike others of his kind he was born human sized. Ashamed of this, his father hid him away. Odin, the ruler of Asgard, discovered baby Loki after killing Loki's father in a massive battle, and took the boy back to Asgard to raise as his son.

This made Loki the brother of Thor. As the two boys grew up together, Thor's heroic nature meant that he began to overshadow his brother. Eventually, Loki became jealous of Thor. He started using lies and magical illusions to trick Thor into doing things that he hoped would make Odin angry. However, Odin wasn't fooled, and he often punished Loki for playing his evil games.

Loki never stops causing trouble, both on Earth and in Asgard. His intelligence and his talent for sorcery make him a dangerous foe. He can change shape, fly and even travel into different dimensons. His hatred of Thor now extends to all the Avengers, who have helped Thor defeat him many times.

HERO VERSUS MISFIT
THOR AND LOKI

THOR

Odin sent his son Thor to live on Earth as a human. Years later, Thor found a walking stick. It changed into Mjolnir – a magic hammer that transformed him back into a god.

Full name: Thor Odinson
Titles: Prince of Asgard, god of thunder
Race: Asgardian
Powers: Super-speed, agility and senses; time travel; ability to regenerate; skilled combatant (assisted by Mjolnir and the Belt of Strength); ability to summon lightning, rain, wind and snow.

LOKI

Odin adopted Loki after the Asgardians killed his father, Laufey. Loki is jealous of Odin's own son, Thor, and has often tried to destroy him.

Full name: Loki Laufeyson
Titles: god of evil, god of mischief
Original race: Frost Giant
Powers: Strength, stamina, speed and intelligence; immunity to physical injury, diseases and toxins; telepathy, hypnosis; ability to travel through time and space; flight through levitation; expert shapeshifter.

The sinister Baron Zemo was another villain with a longstanding grudge against an Avengers member. His hatred of Captain America endured for decades. The two first met during World War II, when Zemo was one of Nazi Germany's top weapons inventors. Zemo had created the world's strongest glue, Adhesive X, which he planned to use as a weapon. Captain America destroyed the huge vat of glue, unaware that Zemo was standing near the vat. The Adhesive X spilled onto Zemo's head, permanently gluing his pink mask to his face!

Zemo swore revenge. When Captain America

and his pal Bucky
tried to stop him
from stealing an
experimental drone
plane, Zemo got his
chance. He tied the
heroes to the plane,
which was loaded
with explosives, and
launched them to
their doom. Decades
later, a furious Zemo
learned that
Captain America
had survived and

had been revived by the Avengers.

Zemo went on to form a Super Villain
group called the Masters of Evil to help him
defeat the Avengers. He never saw victory.
During a battle with the Avengers, Zemo
was killed in an avalanche he caused while
trying to shoot Captain America.

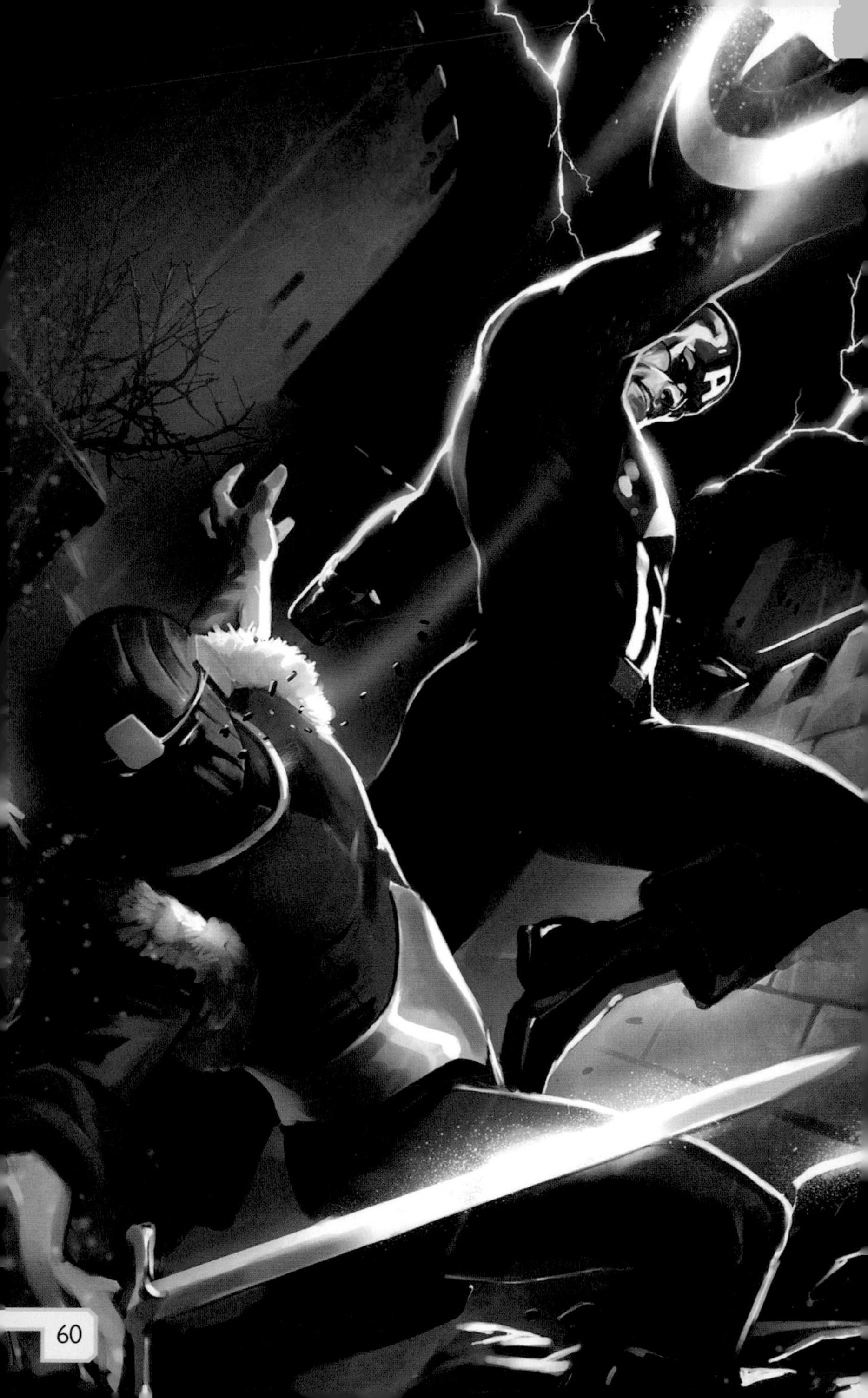

Zemo's son later took his father's place as Baron Zemo. The new Zemo blamed Captain America for the death of his father, and he formed a new Masters of Evil to fight the Avengers. He had the villains pretend to be a team of heroes called the Thunderbolts, hoping that they would become more popular than the Avengers. However, the plan fell apart when some of them chose to become real heroes. Undaunted, Baron Zemo formed a third Masters of Evil.

Another evil group that the Avengers have faced many times is an organisation called Hydra, whose aim is to conquer the world. Hydra takes its name from a snake-like monster in Greek myths that had many heads. Every time one of the monster's heads was cut off, two more would grow in its place, so it could never be destroyed.

Members of Hydra believe that for every agent that is defeated, two more will always continue their mission. Hydra agents usually work undercover, hiding their identities from the world as they carry out their evil plans. Their secret missions can last for years.

Hydra has had several villainous leaders over the years, and one of the most dangerous was Baron Strucker. The top Nazi officer seized command of Hydra after the end of World War II, and used the organisation to cause chaos for many years. A more recent leader of Hydra is the sinister Madame Hydra. This green-haired villain is an expert on poisons and a highly skilled criminal. She relishes the chance to lead a group that is as evil as she.

The Avengers have foiled Hydra's plans time and again, often helped by the UN security force S.H.I.E.L.D. However, like the Greek monster it was named after, Hydra remains impossible to destroy.

Another member of Hydra who has been a great threat to the Avengers is the Red Skull. This evil Nazi officer once wore a terrifying red mask, but an accident with a toxic powder turned his face into a real red skull! In fact, this powder is one of his deadliest weapons. When the "dust of death" hits its victim, it turns their head into a skull – no one can survive it.

During the war, the Red Skull and Captain America fought many times. Like Cap, the Skull was believed to have died during the war, only to be revived years later. The Nazis may have been defeated, but the Skull wasted no time in returning to his evil ways. Whether he works alone or with other villains, he never stops trying to take over the world. Once, he infiltrated the US government and unleashed a plague so he could control the country. Fortunately, the mighty Avengers were able to stop him.

THE RED SKULL

Created by the evil Nazi dictator Hitler, Red Skull is driven by his hatred of all humanity. Terrorism, intimidation, criminal activity, spreading deadly diseases – he will stop at nothing in his thirst for power.

"AND NOW A TOAST... TO UNENDING CONQUEST!"

"I, WHO AM THE PRINCE OF VILLAINY, SERVE NONE!"

"FREEDOM IS ONLY FOR THE ONE WHO RULES! ALL OTHERS MUST BE SLAVES!"

Kang the Conqueror's evil career has lasted even longer than the Red Skull's. By using time travel technology, Kang has battled the Avengers in many different eras.

Kang was born in the 31st century. After discovering time travel, the villain travelled back to ancient Egypt and used his own technology to rule as the great Pharaoh Rama-Tut. He enjoyed having all this power!

However, conquering just one age would never be enough for Kang. Wearing a costume fitted with a protective force field, he travelled to the Avengers' time. When he demanded every government in the world surrender to him, the Avengers assembled to stop him. Although they defeated him that day, they had no idea that they would have to face him again and again.

One of the Avengers' greatest allies against Kang has been an older version of Kang named Immortus. Immortus was unhappy with how his life had turned out, so he travelled back in time to convince his younger self to change his ways. However, Kang refused to listen, and he still causes the Avengers trouble every chance he gets!

Kang is obsessed with mastering time, but it is death that fascinates the mad Titan Thanos. The monstrous villain is obsessed with causing as much chaos and destruction as possible. He is one of the Avengers' most powerful – and terrifying – enemies.

Thanos was born on Saturn's moon, Titan, where his purple skin and deformed chin caused his people to shun him. This rejection turned him into a twisted and cruel being with no respect for life. He set out to kill as many people as he could by

assembling a vast interstellar navy to destroy their worlds. To aid his warriors, Thanos hunted for strange and powerful weapons like the powerful Infinity Gauntlet.

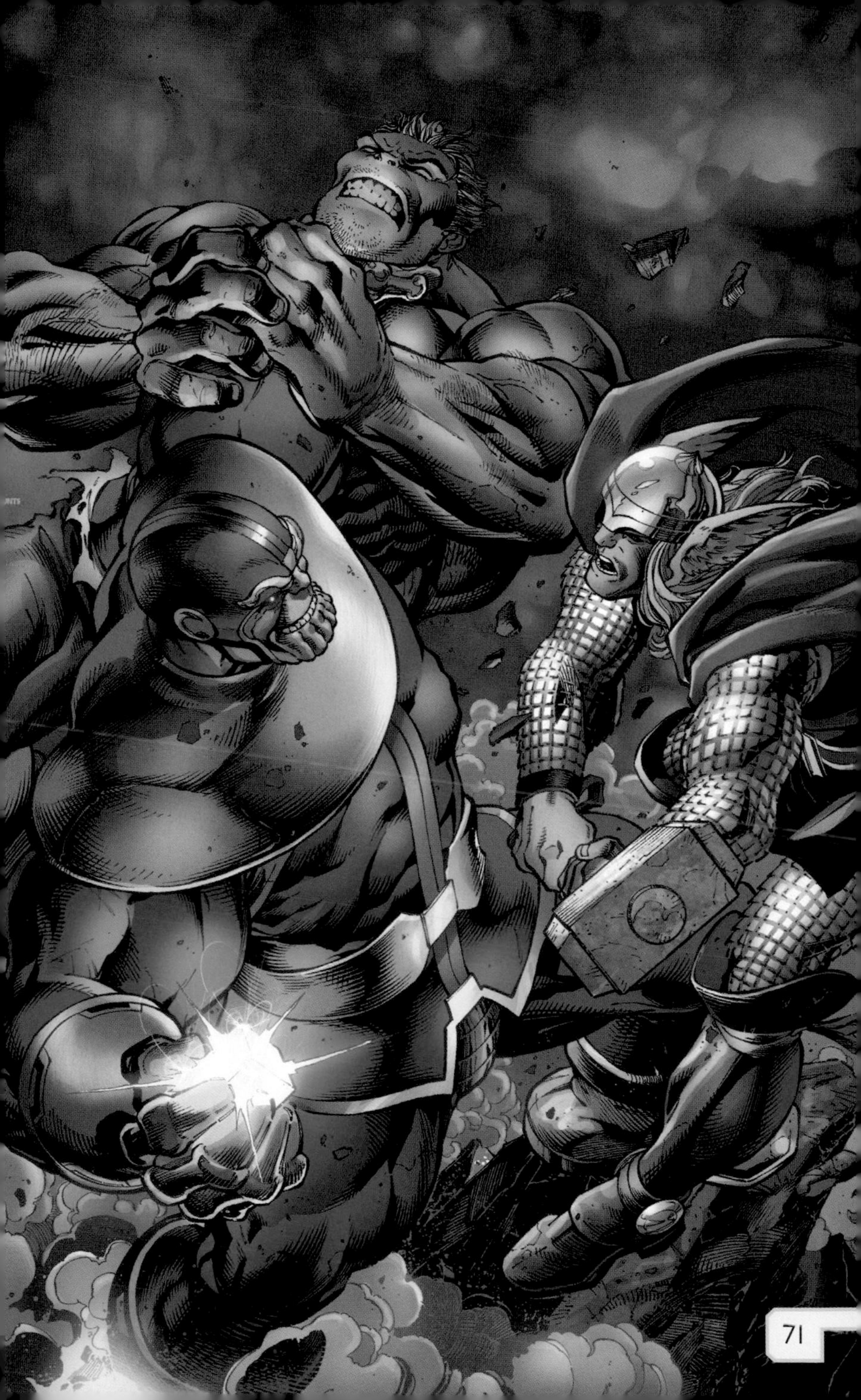

ARCH-ENEMIES

Every once in a while, a Super Hero meets his match – an enemy who can punch just as hard, has more gadgets and refuses to go away! In these cases, you can never guess who will win. Will it be the Super Hero or the villain?

CAPTAIN AMERICA

Vital Stats: 1.87 metres / 99.75 kg (6 ft 2 in / 220 lbs)
Skills: Super strength, incredible speed, martial arts expert, master battle planner
Weapon of choice: Virtually indestructible shield

RED SKULL

Vital Stats: 1.85 metres / 88.5 kg (6 ft 1 in / 195 lbs)
Skills: Hand-to-hand combat, superb marksman, expert at strategy
Weapon of choice: Dust of death (destroys the victim and makes them look like Red Skull).

THE HULK

Vital Stats: 2.13 metres / 521.75 kg
(7 ft / 1,150 lbs)
Skills: Almost unlimited strength,
ability to leap several miles in one
bound, can create shock waves by
slamming his hands together.
Weapon of Choice: Fists

ABOMINATION

Vital Stats: 2 metres / 444.5 kg (6
feet 8 in / 980 lbs)
Skills: Almost unlimited strength,
can leap several miles in one bound,
resistant to extreme temperature,
can hold his breath for long periods.
Weapon of choice: Fists

IRON MAN

Vital Stats: 1.85 metres / 102 kg
(6 feet 1 inch / 225 lbs)
Skills: Genius, inventor, weapons
expert, business skills
Weapon of choice: The Iron Man
suit, which he upgrades to deal with
different situations

MANDARIN

Vital Stats: 1.9 metres / 97.5 kg
(6 ft 2 in / 215 lbs)
Skills: Brilliant athlete, expert
swordsman, skilled at all forms of
martial arts, genius with earthly
and extra-terrestrial technology.
Weapon of choice: Makluan rings

The Infinity Gauntlet is a golden glove
that allows the wearer to use the six Infinity
Gems, giving him or her vast and
unstoppable power. Thanos once used it to
erase half the living things in the universe.
Even the Avengers couldn't stop him.

His campaign of cruelty only ended when his granddaughter, Nebula, stole the gauntlet. She wanted to use it to gain power for herself, but she was tricked by the Avengers' friend Adam Warlock into reversing the damage done by Thanos.

Defeated and humbled, Thanos seemed to no longer be a threat. However, he soon returned to his evil ways, attacking Earth with a new alien navy called the Black Order. Unfortunately, when Thanos arrived, most of the Avengers were away fighting an alien invasion in deep space. Once they returned home, they wasted no time kicking Thanos and his navy off the planet for good.

Like Thanos, the evil robot Ultron came into the world as an innocent but then gave in to hate. He was built by Ant-Man, who wanted a robot to help him in his lab. It didn't take long for the robot to turn against its maker – and the Avengers.

The Avengers have nearly destroyed Ultron several times, but he always returns in a new and upgraded version. His face now looks like that of a giant, angry bug, and his shell is made of Adamantium, the strongest metal in the world.

Ant-Man used his own brain patterns as the template for Ultron's computerised mind. This gave the robot the emotions of a human, but without a human's sense of right and wrong. Ultron has used brainwashing to make Ant-Man forget about creating him, and to persuade other heroes to fight for him, too.

A portable nuclear engine powers Ultron, its heat making his eyes and mouth glow. He is super-fast and super-strong, and can fly and shoot glowing beams of energy from his hands and eyes. He can also control other computers remotely, on one occasion even taking over Iron Man's armour!

Recently, Ultron has started building copies of himself, so the Avengers now have an army of Ultrons to contend with. It is one the greatest challenges the Avengers have ever faced – but if anyone is ready for a challenge, it is Earth's Mightiest Heroes!

ULTRON
THROUGH THE AGES

Ultron is a super-intelligent robot whose mission is to destroy life on Earth and replace it with machines. He has had many battles with the Avengers, rebuilding and upgrading himself each time he is defeated.

ULTRON 1

Dr Hank Pym created Ultron-1 when he was experimenting with intelligent robots. Ultron rebelled against Hank and brainwashed him into forgetting his existence. The robot then began to upgrade himself.

CRIMSON COWL

As upgrade Ultron-5, the robot disguised himself as the Crimson Cowl and formed a group of Super Villains called the New Masters of Evil.

ULTRON 6

From Ultron-6 onwards, the robot's body was made of Admantium – an indestructible metal that can only be pierced by bullets made of the same material.

ULTRON 17 (SIEGE)

Evil robot Ultron-17 trapped Hank Pym in another dimension, leaving a divided Avengers team without anyone to lead them. Ultron intended to kill his creator, but Hank managed to escape.

GREAT ULTRON, RULER OF THE PHALANX

After one defeat, Ultron's consciousness escaped his body and travelled through space. He came across a group of evil cyborgs called the Phalanx and became their leader.

ULTRON WARS

Ultron returned to Earth in the body of a Galadorian Spaceknight and went on to defeat most of the world's Super Heroes.

AGE OF ULTRON

After Ultron defeated most of the Super Heroes, the fate of the world hung in the balance. To save mankind, Wolverine and the Invisible Woman use time travel to go back to the past. They asked Hank Pym to create a code to stop the evil robot. This code destroyed Ultron and saved the world.

Locations

The main headquarters for the Avengers has always been in one of the biggest and brightest places in America: New York City!

When the Avengers' journey as a team of heroes began, their very first headquarters was Avengers Mansion. This beautiful brick building is owned by Tony Stark, who generously turned it into a home for the team. Tony's loyal butler, Edwin Jarvis, took great pride in looking after the Mansion and

helping the Avengers – even if it sometimes meant getting caught up in their adventures!

The Mansion looked grand from the outside, but that was nothing compared to what was inside. Behind those old brick walls lay totally modern and awesome technology. The high-tech headquarters had three hidden underground floors containing everything an Avenger could need, including a fully equipped gym, space for battle training, secret meeting rooms and advanced laboratories.

The Avengers' reputation kept most criminals away, but the Mansion was still protected by high walls and several hidden security devices.

Any Super Villains tempted to break into the Mansion would quickly find themselves in trouble!

However, an attack on the Mansion was eventually successful. Baron Zemo and the Masters of Evil destroyed it during a fierce battle, reducing it to ruins. The Avengers worked hard to rebuild the Mansion, but after several other attacks over the years, they decided it would be a wise move to abandon the place for a new home.

Once again, quick-thinking Tony Stark was happy to provide the team with a new headquarters in his incredible skyscraper, Stark Tower. The Avengers moved into the top three floors, and their new headquarters soon became known as Avengers Tower.

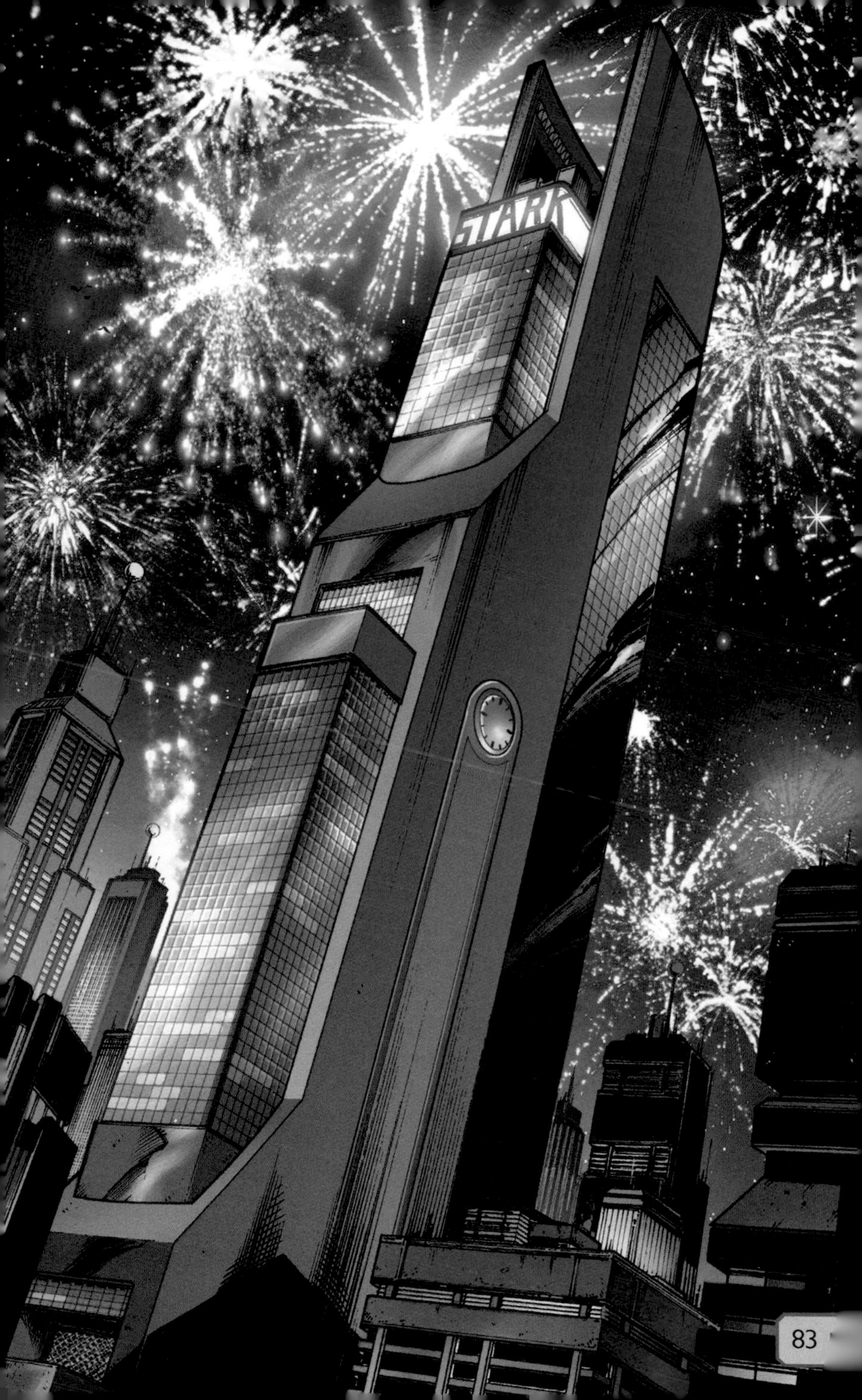
STARK

Unlike the Mansion, Avengers Tower is modern both inside and out. Because of the constant threat of attack, Tony is always looking for way to protect the Avengers living there. Thanks to his love of technology, the Tower's walls have been reinforced with Vibranium, and the windows are virtually unbreakable.

However, Avengers Tower has still been damaged many times – and not only by Super Villains! It almost collapsed during a violent battle between Iron Man and the Hulk.

The tower was seriously damaged a second time during a massive war between Thor and his uncle Cul, who had broken out of a prison to try to conquer the world.

The Avengers came together from places near and far. Although they all use Avengers Tower as their headquarters, not every Avenger prefers to live there – and not just because it can be such a dangerous address. Heroes like Captain America and Hawkeye sometimes spend time in their own apartments in nearby Brooklyn. Some of the heroes who have families prefer to go home to them. Others have been known to retreat to other worlds entirely.

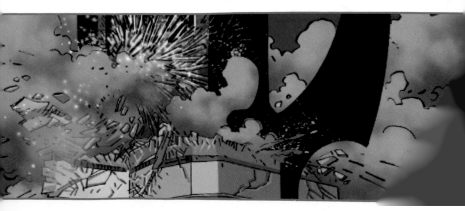

AVENGERS ASSEMBLE

The Avengers are based in New York City, but they have links to many other locations around the world.

NEW YORK CITY
The site of Avengers Mansion and the Avengers Tower are situated in New York City, USA.

NORTH ATLANTIC OCEAN
The body of Captain America was discovered in a block of ice in the North Atlantic Ocean.

NEW MEXICO
Bruce Banner was transformed into the Hulk in New Mexico, USA. He was hit by radioactive particles while developing a bomb at a missile base.

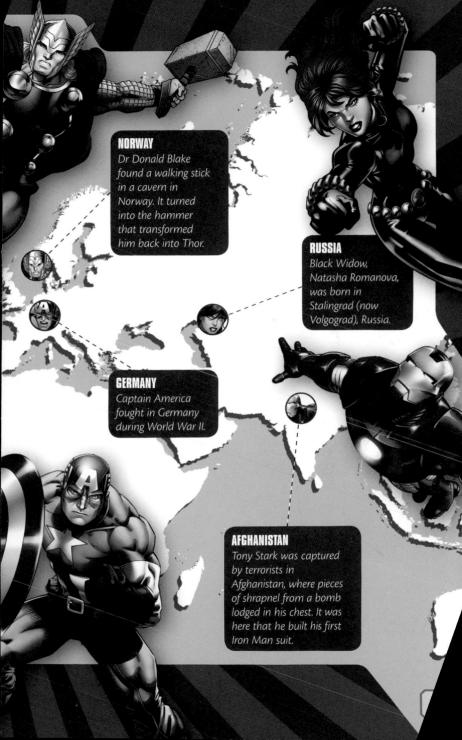

NORWAY
Dr Donald Blake found a walking stick in a cavern in Norway. It turned into the hammer that transformed him back into Thor.

RUSSIA
Black Widow, Natasha Romanova, was born in Stalingrad (now Volgograd), Russia.

GERMANY
Captain America fought in Germany during World War II.

AFGHANISTAN
Tony Stark was captured by terrorists in Afghanistan, where pieces of shrapnel from a bomb lodged in his chest. It was here that he built his first Iron Man suit.

Thor comes from the kingdom of Asgard, a mystical world that floats in space. When he is not working with the Avengers, he often returns home to be with his own people and to help his father, Odin, with ruling the kingdom. This small but mighty realm is home to super-powered Asgardians, and its huge cliffs and waterfalls make it a beautiful place to live. The kingdom's magnificent city

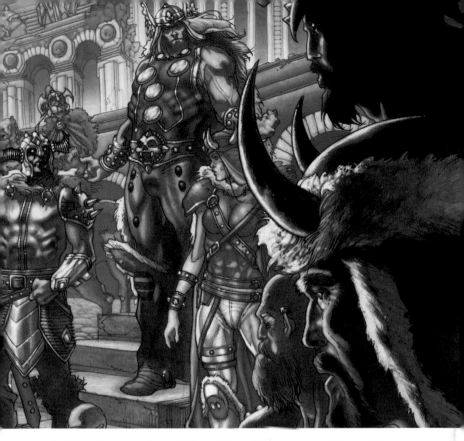

is full of grand, golden buildings with tall, spiralling towers.

Asgard may be far from Earth, but Thor is always ready to rejoin the Avengers when he is needed. The two worlds are connected by an incredible Rainbow Bridge – also called the Bifrost – so whenever Thor must return to his fellow Avengers, he can use it to quickly travel back to Earth.

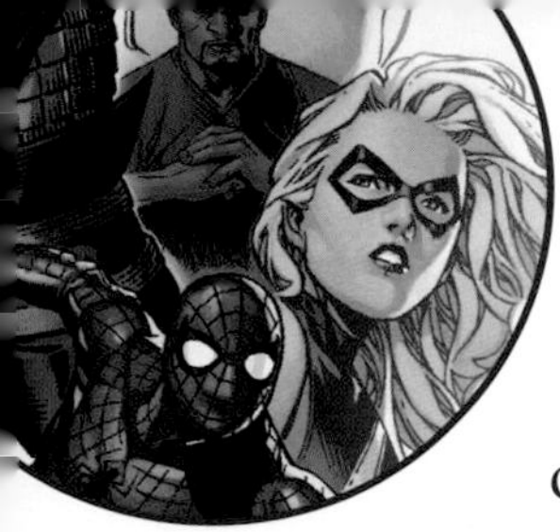

A Changing Roster

The Avengers are made up of a group of core heroes, but the team has had anywhere from four members to dozens of members at a time. The team has sometimes even broken up into separate squads so they can handle many missions at once. Even heroes with long histories of working alone have answered the call to join Earth's Mightiest Heroes!

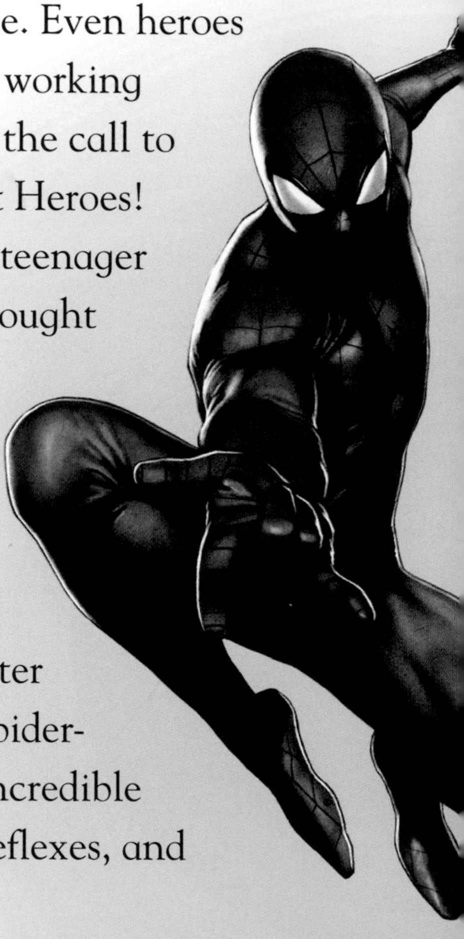

Quiet and skinny teenager Peter Parker never thought he'd be asked to join any team, much less the Avengers. However, after being bitten by a radioactive spider, Peter gained a number of spider-like powers. He has incredible strength, speed and reflexes, and he can stick to and climb any surface. Peter also has a special spider-sense that tells him when he's in danger, and he has invented web shooters that fire sticky webs. He can use the webs to swing into action through the streets of New York, and to trap criminals.

The Avengers invited Spider-Man to join them early in his career. To test his abilities, they asked him to bring them the Hulk, who was not an Avenger at the time. When Spidey discovered that the Hulk was also Bruce Banner, he refused to capture an innocent man. He told the team he had failed the test, and continued to work alone. Spider-Man still helped the Avengers several times over the years, and he became friends with many of its team members.

Spidey eventually became an official
Avenger when he helped the team try to stop
a jailbreak from the Raft, a prison for world's
most dangerous Super Villains. He has
quickly become an important
and much-loved member.
Around the same
time that Spider-Man
officially joined the
Avengers, a hero
named Luke Cage
caught the attention of
the team. As a young
man, Luke was known as
Carl Lucas, and he was
thrown into prison for a
crime he did not commit.
He was desperate to find
a way out, so he
volunteered to be
a test subject for a
new version of the

Super-Soldier Serum. The serum made Carl super-strong and made his skin so tough that bullets bounced straight off him. After using his new strength to escape from prison, Carl changed his name to Luke Cage and became a "Hero

for Hire". He would use his powers to help anyone who could pay his price.

Luke was at the Raft prison, working as a bodyguard, when the jailbreak there started. His heroic actions earned the respect of Captain America that night, and the next morning Cap invited Luke to be part of the new Avengers team. Luke has since shown a real talent for leadership, and is often in charge of smaller squads of Avengers.

COULD YOU BE AN AVENGER?

The Avengers are looking for a new member to join their team of heroes and help them in their fight against evil. Applicants wishing to apply for the job must have some of the following skills or experience:

Superb combat skills, extreme strength, speed and endurance

Ability to invent or use the best technology

Experience of travelling through time and throughout the universe

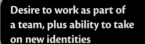
Desire to work as part of a team, plus ability to take on new identities

Commitment to the cause, and willingness to always meet the call to assemble

The Avengers are equal-opportunity employers. Applicants from any background, gender or species are welcome.

New members must be prepared to work with S.H.I.E.L.D. and other law enforcement agencies.

DO YOU HAVE WHAT IT TAKES TO JOIN EARTH'S MIGHTIEST HEROES?

Colonel Carol Danvers has always been a natural leader, too. Carol was a talented fighter pilot for the US Air Force when she met the original Captain Marvel, a warrior from the alien Kree race. When the two of them were caught in an explosion, she gained his incredible powers. She decided to use her new abilities to become a Super Hero, calling herself Ms Marvel. After the original Captain Marvel died, Carol took on his name, and she has certainly lived up to the title.

Carol is super-strong and fast, and she can survive in outer space. She can

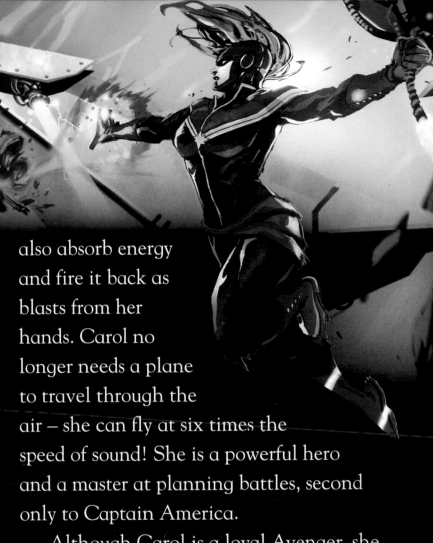

also absorb energy
and fire it back as
blasts from her
hands. Carol no
longer needs a plane
to travel through the
air – she can fly at six times the
speed of sound! She is a powerful hero
and a master at planning battles, second
only to Captain America.

Although Carol is a loyal Avenger, she
often leaves the team to have adventures of
her own. She enjoys exploring space, but she
always returns. She has even led her own
squad of the Avengers, and she has become
an important part of the expanded team.

Just like Captain Marvel, the Falcon has joined and left the Avengers many times. However, whenever they need him most, he always answers their call.

Before becoming a hero, Sam Wilson was a small-time crook, nicknamed "Snap" Wilson. While working for the mob, he became caught up in one of the Red Skull's villainous plans to destroy Captain America. The Skull gave Sam the ability to communicate with Sam's pet falcon, Redwing. He then brainwashed Sam into becoming the Falcon, intending to have him befriend Cap, only to betray him later. However, Sam's good nature overcame his brainwashing and the Falcon became a true hero!

Ever since then, the Falcon has only used his powers for good, acting as Cap's loyal crime-fighting partner. He wears a large set of jet-powered wings that allow him to fly. When it comes to combat in the air, his skills exceed even those of Iron Man.

Sam has joined Cap in the Avengers many times over the years. He has even taken over as Captain America at a time when the original Cap (Steve Rogers) was unable to continue fighting.

S.H.I.E.L.D.

The Strategic Hazard Intervention, Espionage and Logistic Directorate is better known by its initials: S.H.I.E.L.D. The US government set up S.H.I.E.L.D. after World War II to deal with the threat from the international criminal organisation known as Hydra. Today, S.H.I.E.L.D. has a much bigger mission: to protect the world from villains of any kind. To do this, it relies on cutting-edge technology and a core of experienced and determined spies.

S.H.I.E.L.D. requires its agents to be available for action wherever they are needed, so it has its headquarters on a gigantic floating fortress known as the Helicarrier.

Many Avengers have been members of
S.H.I.E.L.D. in the past, including Captain
America and Black Widow. Because the two
organisations have a shared goal – to save
the world – they often work together. When
S.H.I.E.L.D. discovers trouble it can't handle
alone, it passes the information it has to the
Avengers. They stop the villains and, if
they're lucky, capture them and turn them
over to S.H.I.E.L.D. for questioning.

S.H.I.E.L.D. HELICARRIER

The Helicarrier is the mobile headquarters for the peace-keeping organisation called S.H.I.E.L.D. It can travel on water and also fly. As well as being a base for fighters and other aircraft, it is packed with advanced weapons.

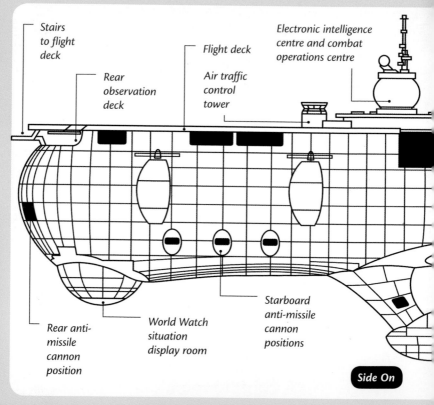

Stairs to flight deck

Rear observation deck

Flight deck

Air traffic control tower

Electronic intelligence centre and combat operations centre

Rear anti-missile cannon position

World Watch situation display room

Starboard anti-missile cannon positions

Side On

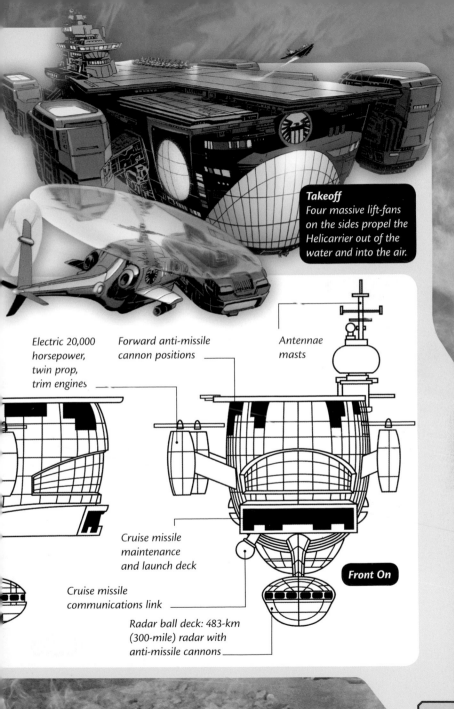

Takeoff
Four massive lift-fans on the sides propel the Helicarrier out of the water and into the air.

Electric 20,000 horsepower, twin prop, trim engines

Forward anti-missile cannon positions

Antennae masts

Cruise missile maintenance and launch deck

Cruise missile communications link

Front On

Radar ball deck: 483-km (300-mile) radar with anti-missile cannons

The relationship between the Avengers and S.H.I.E.L.D. demands complete trust. Fortunately, S.H.I.E.L.D.'s director is an old ally of Captain America: the legendary Nick Fury. The two American heroes have been close friends since they fought alongside each other in World War II.

During the war, Nick led an elite unit of US Army soldiers known as the Howling Commandos. They took on highly dangerous missions, clashing frequently with the vicious Nazi commander Baron Strucker, who later became the leader of the evil organisation, Hydra.

Nick's famous black eye patch is a result of his experiences during the war. He wears it to cover his left eye, which was badly damaged in an explosion.

Nick helped to set up S.H.I.E.L.D., and he served as its director for decades. Even after he left the job, Nick continued to work to save the world, although he operated undercover and without official permission.

While running S.H.I.E.L.D.,
Nick Fury had a child with a
fellow agent, Nia Jones.
Nia feared that the boy
would become a target for
S.H.I.E.L.D.'s enemies. She
decided to raise him alone,
changing her last name to
Johnson to hide their identity.
The boy, Marcus, grew up
with no memory of his father, yet he took
after him, even joining the US Army.

After serving in the Middle East, Marcus returned home and was thrown back into his father's world when he became caught up in a battle between Nick Fury and a Russian villain named Orion. Marcus helped Fury to defeat Orion, but lost his left eye in the process.

When Marcus finally learned who his father was, he joined S.H.I.E.L.D. and took the name Nick Fury, Jr. He now works as S.H.I.E.L.D.'s primary agent, managing a secret squad of Avengers alongside his ex-army friend Phil Coulson.

Nick Jr and Phil both report to
S.H.I.E.L.D.'s current director, Maria Hill.
Maria took over S.H.I.E.L.D. right after
Nick Fury left the job. Tough but fair, Maria
commands the respect of every S.H.I.E.L.D.
agent. Her intelligence, cool head and sheer

hard work enabled her to
rise through S.H.I.E.L.D.'s
ranks very quickly.

Sometimes other
directors take on the
leadership of S.H.I.E.L.D.
for a while. These include

Captain America and Iron Man. The heroes always return to the Avengers, though, and when they do, Maria resumes her role as regular director.

Sharon Carter is another important person in S.H.I.E.L.D.'s ranks. Growing up, Sharon was thrilled by her aunt Peggy's tales of fighting alongside Captain America during World War II. She decided to follow a similar career by joining S.H.I.E.L.D.

Sharon became one of S.H.I.E.L.D.'s best field agents – Agent 13. She often works so deep undercover that even S.H.I.E.L.D does not know whether she is alive or dead!

When she's not undercover, Sharon is proud to work alongside heroes like Captain America and the other Avengers.

The Avengers Versus Ultron!

Ultron is one of the most dangerous foes that the Avengers have ever faced. Ever since he was created by Hank Pym, Ultron has been obsessed with destroying his creator, along with the rest of the Avengers.

The team has clashed with the evil robot many times, and must always be ready to stop his plans to take over the world. Ultron constantly upgrades himself, so that he can become stronger and more terrifying than ever. He can also brainwash people into rebuilding him if he is destroyed. Therefore, no matter how many times the Avengers defeat him, he always finds a way to return.

During Ultron's early experiences with fighting the Avengers, he realised that they were too powerful for him to defeat alone.

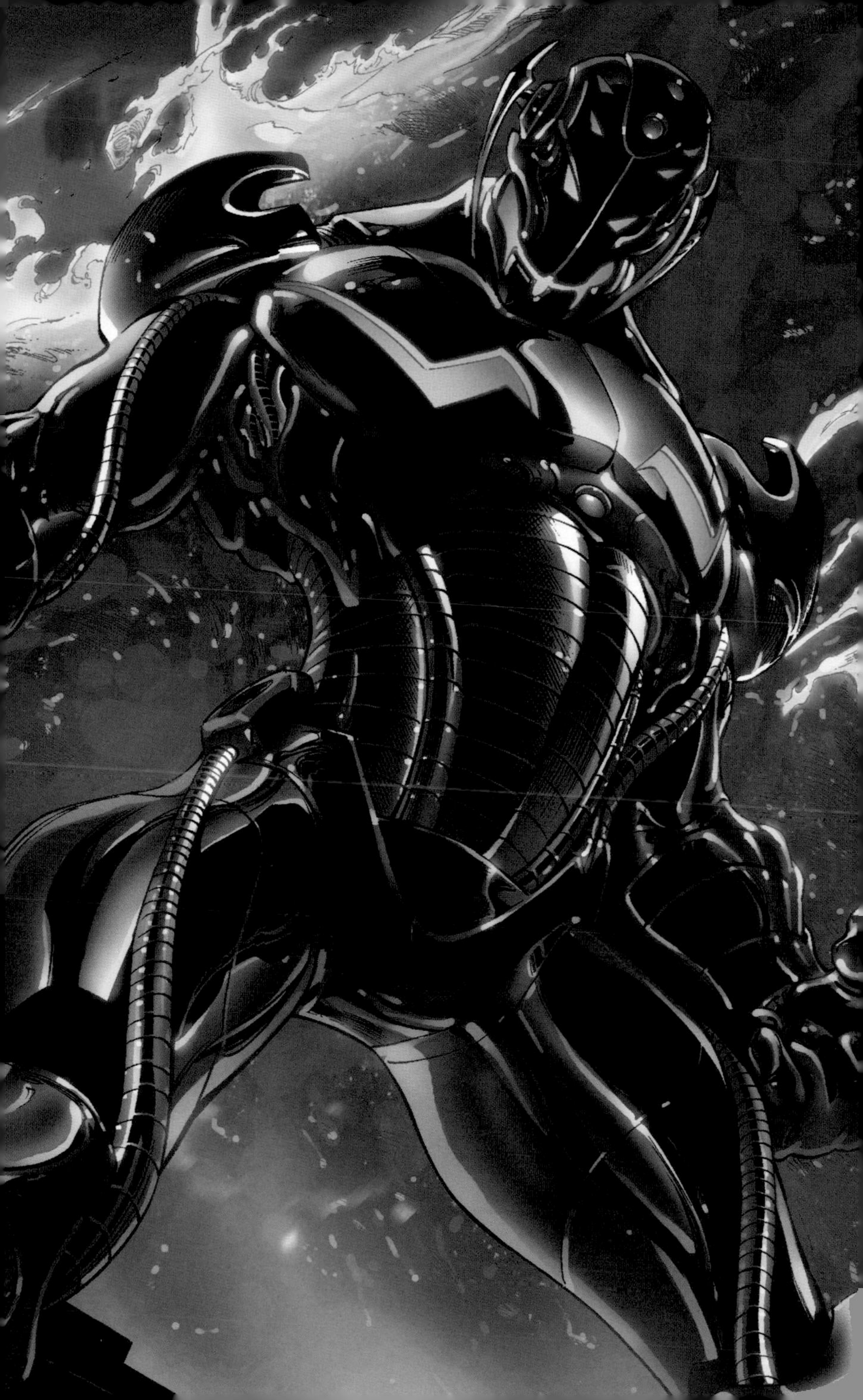

He disguised himself as a criminal called the Crimson Cowl, and led a new Masters of Evil group. However, they were no match for the Avengers, and Ultron's plan failed.

After his defeat, Ultron decided to only rely on his own intelligence, rather than other villains. As time went by he grew stronger, and the Avengers had to battle against the evil robot many times. It didn't take long for the heroes to realise that Ultron was becoming one of their most powerful enemies!

There have been times when Ultron has tried to create other robots as part of his evil plans. However, this has led to more complications than Ultron expected. He created an android he named Vision to attack the Avengers, only to have his creation betray him by becoming an Avenger himself! The two were now enemies.

Ultron's next creation was a female robot named Jocasta. She quickly turned on him and, like Vision, joined the Avengers. The next robot, Alkhema, was just as evil as Ultron, but she too betrayed her creator.

Despite having his plans ruined by each of his creations, Ultron refused to admit defeat. He tried to use Iron Man's technology to his own advantage by attaching his own head to a suit of Iron Man's armour. When this failed, he tried to take control of Iron Man's entire body, as well his armour, and launch missiles that could destroy the world.

ULTRON AND THE AVENGERS TEAM

Evil robot Ultron was the creation of Dr Hank Pym (aka Ant-Man). He rebelled against his creator and quickly became the arch-enemy of the Avengers and the genius who created him.

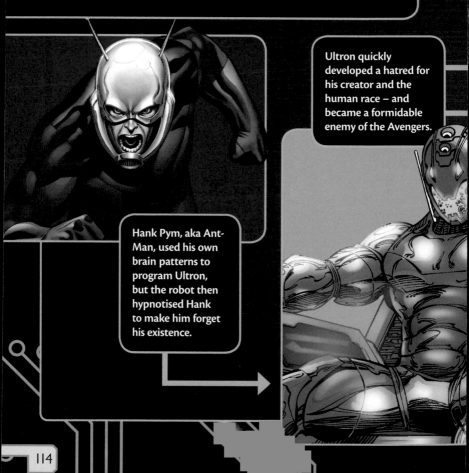

Ultron quickly developed a hatred for his creator and the human race – and became a formidable enemy of the Avengers.

Hank Pym, aka Ant-Man, used his own brain patterns to program Ultron, but the robot then hypnotised Hank to make him forget his existence.

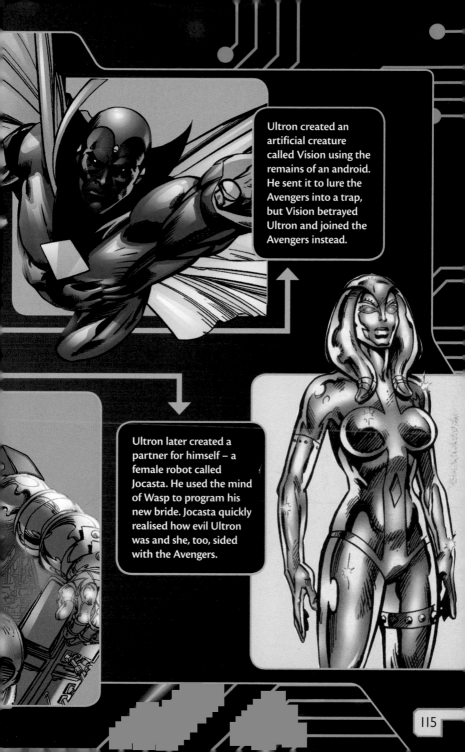

Ultron created an artificial creature called Vision using the remains of an android. He sent it to lure the Avengers into a trap, but Vision betrayed Ultron and joined the Avengers instead.

Ultron later created a partner for himself – a female robot called Jocasta. He used the mind of Wasp to program his new bride. Jocasta quickly realised how evil Ultron was and she, too, sided with the Avengers.

The Avengers managed to stop him, but the worst was yet to come.

Just months later, Ultron launched a terrible plan to destroy humankind by creating copies of himself – the Ultron Sentinels. When he had enough copies to form a huge army, he sent them to take over Earth. The Sentinels destroyed the entire world, defeating almost every Super Hero that stood in their way. The few that managed to survive were forced to watch Ultron transform New York City into a terrifying and dangerous place.

Ultron knew that the Avengers would try to find a way to stop him, so while the Sentinels attacked, he time-travelled into the future. That way, he would always be ready to stop any plans to defeat him.

However, the Avengers realised that if Ultron used time travel to win his battles, then so could they! They came up with a plan to send one team of heroes into the future, so that they could attack Ultron there. They also sent another team into the past, to stop Hank Pym from ever inventing Ultron. If just one team was successful, then the whole world could be saved!

Iron Man, Captain America and the team arrive in the future to join in the ultimate battle against sinister robot Ultron.

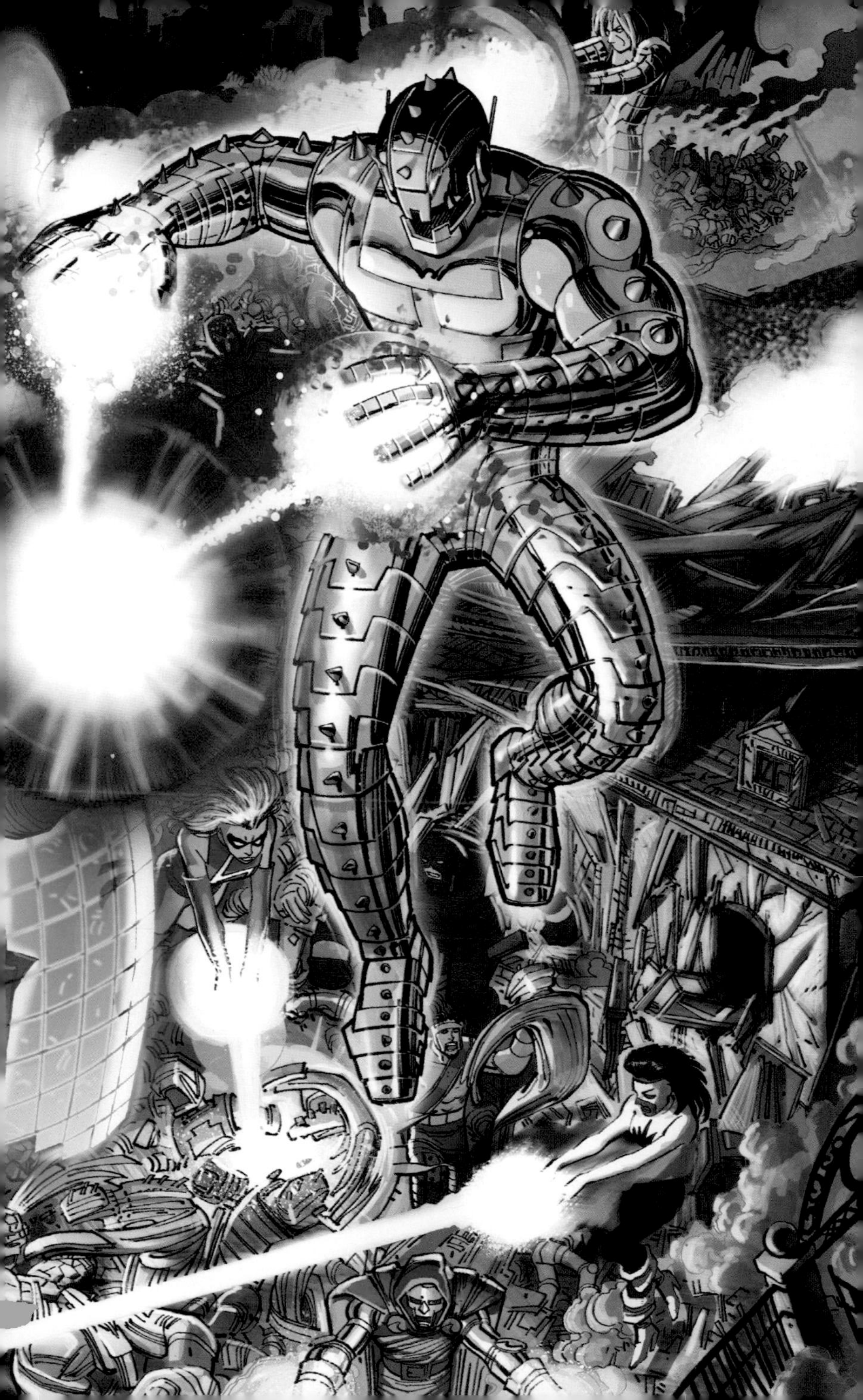

Time travel turned out to be more complicated than the heroes expected. The team that went into the past were able to stop Ultron from being created, but their actions only made things worse. When they returned to the present, they found that the world was far more dark and twisted than the one they remembered.

However, the heroes refused to give up, and they travelled into the past once again.

This time, they convinced Hank to still create Ultron, but to also come up with a way to stop him. Before Ultron could carry out his terrible plans, Hank was ready for him. With some help from Iron Man, he uploaded a virus that shut Ultron down and destroyed him. The Sentinels were never created, and the world was finally safe.

The Avengers may have stopped Ultron's worst attack, but they know that he will not stay defeated forever. One day, the evil robot may return.

Quiz

1. Who came up with the name the "Avengers"?

2. Which member of the Avengers created Ultron?

3. In which country was Tony Stark injured and captured by warlords?

4. With what can Vision's brain communicate?

5. Captain America's shield is made out of which material?

6. What is the name of the group of Super Villains led by Baron Zemo?

7. When Kang began travelling in time, what was the first age he conquered?

8. Where was the evil villain Thanos born?

9. In which city do the Avengers live?

10. How does Thor travel between Asgard and Earth?

11. When did Spider-Man officially become a member of the Avengers?

12. Which Super Hero was originally a fighter pilot?

13. Which Super Villain did Nick Fury fight against, over and over again?

14. Who is currently the director of S.H.I.E.L.D.?

15. How many female robots has Ultron created?

See page 127 for answers.

Glossary

Adamantium
The strongest metal known. It can only be moulded if heated to very high temperatures.

Alien
A creature that comes from somewhere other than planet Earth.

Android
A robot that can look or act like a human being.

Assemble
When a group of people come together in one place.

Brainwashing
Changing or controlling someone's thoughts and actions without them realising.

Combat
A fight or contest between individuals or groups.

Conquer
To take control of something through the use of force.

Cyborg
Someone who is half living being and half machine.

Deep space
Regions of space that are very distant from the Earth and its solar system.

Different dimension
A separate world.

Director
Someone in charge of an organisation who is responsible for making important decisions.

Drone plane
A remote-controlled plane that carries no pilot or crew.

Frost Giants
A race of giants who live in a snowy world called Jotunheim. They are enemies of the Asgardians.

Gamma rays
Invisible rays similar to X-rays but much more powerful.

Headquarters
A place that acts as the centre of a group or organisation.

Indestructible
Impossible to break or destroy.

Infiltrate
To secretly enter or join a group or organisation in order to get information or do them harm.

Interstellar
Travelling in space, among the stars.

Mission
An important task or job that someone is given to do.

Mob
A secret organisation that makes money from crime.

Mutation
A change in the genes that causes someone's physical characteristics to change.

Nazi
Member of a brutal political party that controlled Germany in the 1930s and 1940s.

Particles
Units of matter or energy.

Plague
A deadly, highly infectious disease that spreads quickly and affects a lot of people.

Portable
Easy to move or carry around.

Radioactive
Having or producing a powerful and dangerous form of energy called radiation.

Shrapnel
Fragments from an exploding bomb.

Steadfast
Firm in purpose and beliefs.

Super Hero
A person with amazing powers or abilities, who fights to protect people and save the world.

Super-Soldier Serum
A special formula that greatly increases a person's physical and mental abilities.

Super Villain
A person with amazing powers or abilities, who does evil things or hurts other people.

Technology
The collection of tools, including machinery, created by humans.

Template
A pattern or guide upon which other things are based.

Toxic
Containing poisonous material.

Undaunted
Not afraid to continue doing something, even though there are problems.

Undercover
Working in a secret way to catch enemies or collect information.

Upgrade
When something is made newer and better.

Vibranium
A rare metal that is very durable and can absorb almost any impact.

World War II
A worldwide war that took place from 1939-1945.

Index

Quiz answers
1. Wasp 2. Hank Pym
3. Afghanistan 4. Computers
5. Vibranium 6. The Masters of Evil 7. Ancient Egypt 8. Titan
9. New York City

10. He uses the Rainbow Bridge (also called the Bifrost) 11. When he helped the Avengers to stop a jailbreak at the Raft prison.
12. Captain Marvel 13. Baron Strucker 14. Maria Hill 15. Two

Have you read these other great books from DK?

READING ALONE

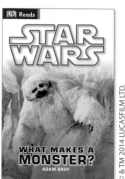

© & TM 2014 LUCASFILM LTD.

© & TM 2014 LUCASFILM LTD.

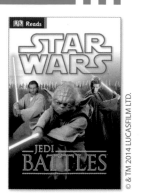

© & TM 2014 LUCASFILM LTD.

Read all about the scariest monsters in the Star Wars galaxy.

Meet the Sith Lords who are trying to take over the galaxy.

Find out all about the brave Jedi Knights and their epic adventures.

Life-or-death futuristic space adventure to find a new home planet.

Pulse-racing action adventure chasing twisters in Tornado Alley.

Time-travelling adventure caught up in the intrigue in ancient Rome.